·Bartholomew·

WALK SOUTH DEVON
COASTAL PATH & DARTMOOR
by John H.N. Mason and Eric Hemery

Bartholomew
A Division of HarperCollins*Publishers*

Published by Bartholomew, a Division of HarperCollins*Publishers*,
12 Duncan Street, Edinburgh EH9 1TA.

Pages 5-10 and 14-38 are based on the South West Peninsula Coast Path
guide books previously published by Letts and compiled by Ken Ward and
John H.N. Mason with maps drawn by Ian Ward.

A catalogue record for this book is available from the British Library.

First Published 1992

Text (pages 5-10, 14-38) © John H.N. Mason 1992
Text (pages 11-13, 39-48) © Eric Hemery 1992
Maps (pages 4, 14-38) © Bartholomew 1992
Maps (pages 39-48) © Harvey Map Services Ltd 1992

HARVEYS

12-16 MAIN STREET DOUNE PERTHSHIRE FK16 6BJ SCOTLAND
TEL: 0786 841202 INTERNATIONAL (44) 786 841202 TELEX 778583

Printed in Great Britain by Bartholomew,
HarperCollins*Manufacturing*, Edinburgh.

ISBN 0 7028 1811 9

Britain's landscape is changing all the time. While every care has
been taken in the preparation of this guide, Bartholomew accepts
no responsibility whatsoever for any loss, damage, injury or inconvenience
sustained or caused as a result of using this guide.

Acknowledgments: John H.N. Mason would like to acknowledge gratefully
the help received from many people but particularly from: Ken Ward,
President, Backpackers' Club; Philip Carter (Chairman) and Eric Wallis
(Hon. Secretary), South West Way Association; Roger Burrows, BA,MIBiol;
Dr Paul Chanin, MA PhD.; Ian Kemp and Richard Butler,
Heritage Coast Officers, c/o Devon County Council, Exeter.

CONTENTS

Key Map to Location of Each Walk

23 — Route of South Devon
～ — Coastal Path
□ — Area covered by each walk

KEY TO ROUTE MAPS
Coastal Path: see P. 6 for symbols
Dartmoor:

— route of walk
---- walking directions
⑧ description of viewpoint
Ⓟ car park
== road
----- track, footpath
▪ □ building, ruin
woodland boundary
ruined boundary
marshy ground
374 heights in metres
river, stream

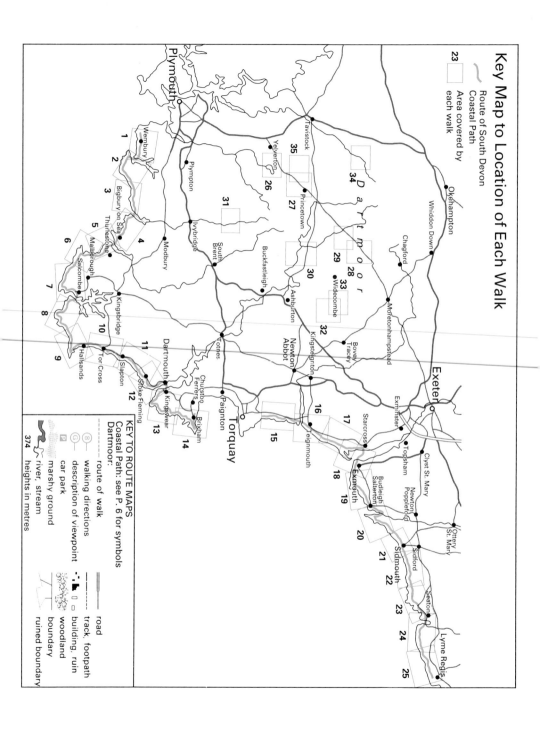

Plymouth
Wembury 1
2
3 Bigbury on Sea
Thurlestone 5
6 Malborough
Salcombe
7
8
Kingsbridge
10
11
12 Stoke Fleming
Slapton
Tor Cross 9
Hallsands
Plympton
Modbury 4
Ivybridge
South Brent
Buckfastleigh
31
Yelverton
Tavistock
35
26
27 Princetown
Dartmoor
34
30
29 33
28
Widecombe
32
Chagford
Whiddon Down
Okehampton
Moretonhampstead
Bovey Tracey
Kingsteignton
Newton Abbot
Ashburton
Totnes
Dartmouth
Kingswear
13
Brixham
14
Churston Ferrers
Paignton
Torquay
15
16
Teignmouth
17
Starcross
Exminster
Exeter
Clyst St. Mary
Topsham
Newton Poppleford
Ottery St. Mary
18
19 Exmouth
Budleigh Salterton
20
Sidford
Sidmouth
21
22
23
Seaton
24
Lyme Regis
25

WALKING IN SOUTH DEVON

South Devon provides some of Britain's very best and most varied walking terrain. In this guide, the entire South Devon Coastal Path is described step-by-step and there are also detailed walks in Dartmoor National Park.

As you enjoy walking these routes, please remember to observe the Country Code in order to safeguard this beautiful terrain:

1. Guard against all risk of fire
2. Fasten all gates
3. Keep dogs under proper control
4. Keep to the paths across farmland
5. Avoid damaging fences, hedges and walls
6. Leave no litter — take it home
7. Safeguard water supplies
8. Protect wildlife, wild plants and trees
9. Go carefully on country roads
10. Respect the life of the countryside

THE SOUTH DEVON COASTAL PATH

The National Parks Act of 1929 provided for a number of long-distance footpaths throughout the country. These are now known as National Trails. The longest of these splendid initiatives is the South-West Coast Path, over 500 miles (800km) long, which runs along the coast from Minehead in Somerset to Poole Harbour in Dorset. This guide describes the stretch on the coast in South Devon.

Most of the South Devon Coast has been designated as one of the 'Heritage Coasts' of England, the area being divided into the South Devon and the East Devon Heritage Coasts. The Countryside Commission, working through the local authorities, appoints 'Heritage Coast Officers' for the region involved. Their aims are conservation and management of the amenities, thus encouraging local people and visitors to care for and enjoy the coasts. For information write to: Heritage Coast Officer, c/o Devon County Council, Amenities Dept, County Hall, Topsham Road, Exeter EX2 4QH.

The South-West Way Association, which furthers the interests of walkers on the Coastal Path, publishes a guide for its members with up to date information on the Path. Details are available from: 1 Orchard Drive, Kingskerswell, Newton Abbot, Devon, TQ12 5DG.

Each part of the route in this guide is graded section by section according to the type of terrain to be covered. Most sections can be negotiated without much difficulty although the elderly and those not so active should consider carefully before tackling the stretches shown as 'strenuous' in the text.

The Path is often stony and narrow and, even on the least strenuous of sections, good, strong, well-tried, comfortable boots are a 'must'. They not only help to maintain a sure-footed grip but, worn with woollen socks, they reduce the risk of blistered feet.

South Devon has a good sunshine record but you should, however, be prepared for rain and wind so lightweight rainwear is important. A loose-fitting waterproof knee-length jacket with a hood should keep you dry. Waterproof over-trousers are also useful. Remember in hot sun keep your head and neck protected. You motto should be 'travel light'.

The footpath route of the South Devon Coastal Path, as shown in green on the Coastal Path route on the maps in this guide, is a public right of way and this also applies to the 'alternative' path(s) shown in a dotted line (also in green). Where there are access paths shown in a dotted black line these are also public rights of way.

Apart from the rights of way indicated above, you must not deviate from the route unless there is another footpath or bridle-way which is clearly marked as such.

In the text on each page, in addition to the instructions to bear in mind when walking the Path,

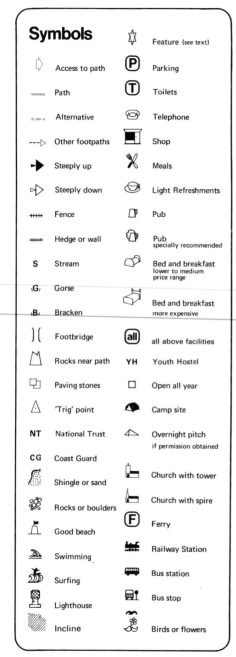

Symbols

🏳	Feature (see text)		
◊	Access to path	(P)	Parking
—	Path	(T)	Toilets
▪▪▪	Alternative	☎	Telephone
---▷	Other footpaths	🏪	Shop
➡	Steeply up	✗	Meals
▷▷	Steeply down	☕	Light Refreshments
++++	Fence	🍺	Pub
∞∞∞	Hedge or wall	🍺	Pub specially recommended
S	Stream	🛏	Bed and breakfast lower to medium price range
,G,	Gorse	🛏	Bed and breakfast more expensive
,B,	Bracken		
)(	Footbridge	(all)	all above facilities
⋀	Rocks near path	YH	Youth Hostel
▦	Paving stones	□	Open all year
△	'Trig' point	⛺	Camp site
NT	National Trust	⛺	Overnight pitch if permission obtained
CG	Coast Guard	🏛	Church with tower
🏖	Shingle or sand	🏛	Church with spire
🪨	Rocks or boulders	(F)	Ferry
🏖	Good beach	🚂	Railway Station
🏊	Swimming	🚌	Bus station
🏄	Surfing	🚌	Bus stop
🗼	Lighthouse	🌸	Birds or flowers
⫻	Incline		

there is also scenic information and observations of the wildlife and historical and archaeological points of interest.

1 FOLLOWING THE COASTAL ROUTE

The purpose of this guide is to enable the reader not only to find his or her way easily and accurately, section by section, along the full length of the South Devon Coastal Path but also to provide additional information in a most convenient form that can be of greatest help in planning and while walking. The sketch maps take the work out of following the Path and navigating your route. Nevertheless a good 1:100 000 map showing the line of the Path is an excellent complement to this guide, especially if you are seeking more detailed information on access or you are interested in leaving the Path for short excursions inland.

The key to symbols used on the maps provides a great deal of invaluable information on types of gradients encountered and facilities available.

Other helpful features are the symbols marking the approximate location of refreshment facilities as well as guest houses, hotels, hostels and camp-sites. The texts accompanying the maps serve to amplify the information on the route itself. The official Path is indicated by a solid green line and alternative paths are shown by a broken green line.

Distances On the right hand side of each map, an indication of approximate mileages is given. At the beginning of each section, the distance to be walked is shown as well as the cumulative distance from Plymouth (Turnchapel). Approximate metric equivalents are also given.

Access to the Path The guide endeavours to cater for everyone with an interest in the Path; the more serious walkers may wish to spend a week or fortnight walking every day, whereas there may be some whose interest extends only to an afternoon's stroll or a day's walk and would therefore prefer to select a particular stretch of the Path. To help in this, the guide includes in the maps the most convenient access points to the Path, indicated by a green arrow. Adjacent car-parking facilities, where available, are also shown.

Bathing This is often dangerous, particularly for children or non-swimmers so pay attention to warning signs and always be guided by flags and lifeguards.

Tides When walking the South-West Coast Path

a knowledge of the state of the tide on a particular day is often useful. On a stretch covered by this book you have to wade an estuary and this can only be done at low tide.

The table given below will enable you, with the help of your newspaper, to determine the approximate time of high and low water. You may also be able to buy local tide tables at newsagents

Most national daily papers give the time of high water at London Bridge (usually beside the weather details). By adding the average time difference in hours and minutes given in the following list you can calculate the time of high water at the places mentioned. For intermediate places the time will be at some time between the two places each side. Low water is approximately 6 hours after high water.

		hrs	mins
Plymouth	Add	3	49
Salcombe	Add	4	10
Dartmouth	Add	4	32
Brixham	Add	4	36
Torquay	Add	4	40
Teignmouth	Add	4	37
Exmouth	Add	4	45

2 ACCOMMODATION, REFRESHMENTS AND INFORMATION

Accommodation The accommodation shown in the guide has been selected for its position close to the Path and its capacity to provide overnight bed and breakfast for walkers. Accommodation has been divided into two price categories (see Symbols p.6). However, when making reservations, always check costs. The telephone number for each establishment is given below and the location has been indicated as near as is possible on the map in relation to the Path. If you have not made an advance reservation, you should decide your target for the following day and then book the nearest accommodation to it. If, for some reason, the guest house, hostel or hotel cannot give lodgings, the proprietor will probably be able to suggest a suitable alternative nearby. Always make clear whether or not an evening meal is required and try to give some indication of expected time of arrival. Two letters on the map after the name of the establishment indicate the period the accommodation is available e.g. AO=April to October, SM=September to March.

□ indicates open throughout the year including the winter months. However, this could be subject to many local variables so it is worth obtaining advance confirmation. On the map, GH=guest house and CS=camp-site.

Refreshments Where possible, an indication is given on the map of where refreshments may be obtained en route. Telephone numbers, where appropriate, are given below. It is worth remembering, however, that many places are only open June to August.

Useful telephone numbers Hotels, guest houses, camp-sites, youth hostels and Tourist Information Offices are shown on the maps (please note that, for some local calls, the code may differ depending on where you are. Check the notice in the telephone box).

Walk

1	Tourist Information, Plymouth	(0752) 264849
	Youth Hostel, Plymouth	(0752) 562189
	Chichester Hotel, Plymouth	(0752) 662746
	Heybrook guest house, Plymouth	(0752) 862345
	Langton Court, Wembury	(0752) 862358
	Bay Cottage, Wembury	(0752) 862559
	River Yealm Hotel, Newton Ferrers	(0752) 872419
4	Trebles Cottage, Kingston	(0548) 810218
	Journey's End Inn, Bigbury	(0548) 810205
	Burgh Island, Bigbury	(0548) 810514
5	Sloop Inn, Bantham	(0548) 560215
	Heron House Hotel, Thurlestone	(0548) 561308
	Hopedene guest house, Hope Cove	(0548) 561602
	Tanfield Hotel, Hope Cove	(0548) 561268
	Hope & Anchor Inn, Hope Cove	(0548) 561294
6	Port Light Hotel, Bolberry Down	(0548) 516613
	Bolberry House Farm camp-site	(0548) 561251
	Soar Mill Cove Hotel	(0548) 561566
	Sun Park camp-site	(0548) 561378
7	Youth Hostel, Salcombe	(0548) 842856
	Tourist Information, Salcombe	(0548) 842736
	Old Porch House, Salcombe	(0548) 842157
8	Gara Rock Hotel	(054884) 2342
10	Cove guest house, Torcross	(0548) 580784
	Venture guest house, Torcross	(0548) 580314
11	Tower Inn, Slapton	(0548) 580216
12	Leonards Cove camp-site,	
	Stoke Fleming	(0803) 770206
	Tourist Information, Dartmouth	(0803) 834224
	Townstall Farm guest house,	
	Dartmouth	(0803) 832300
	Ivanhoe guest house, Dartmouth	(0803) 832591
14	Youth Hostel, Brixham	(0803) 842444
	Orchard House, Brixham	(0803) 853590
	Tourist Information, Brixham	(0803) 852861
	Globe Inn, Brixham	(0803) 852154

	Torhaven Hotel, Brixham	(0803) 882281
15	Tourist Information, Torquay	(0803) 296901
	Dalmeny Hotel, Torquay	(0803) 292936
	Chelston Manor Hotel, Torquay	(0803) 605142
	Palm Court Hotel, Torquay	(0803) 294881
	Mount Nessing Hotel, Torquay	(0803) 292970
16	Coast View Park camp-site, Shaldon	(0626) 872392
	Tourist Information, Teignmouth	(0626) 779769
	Inglewood, Teignmouth	(0626) 293800
	Dresden House, Teignmouth	(0626) 773462
17	Tourist Information, Dawlish	(0626) 863589
	Lamorna Hotel, Dawlish	(0626(862242
	Leadstone camp-site, Dawlish	(0626) 872239
	Peppermint Park camp-site, Dawlish Warren	(0626) 863436
18	Cofton Farm camp-site, Starcross	(0626) 890358
	Tourist Information, Exmouth	(0395) 263744
	Bicton Inn, Exmouth	(0395) 272589
	St Aubyns guest house	(0395) 264069
	Barn Hotel, Exmouth	(0395) 274411
19	Prattshayes Farm camp-site, Sandy Bay	(0395) 276626
20	Tourist Information, Budleigh Salterton	(0395) 445275
	Tidwell House, Budleigh Salterton	(0395) 442444
21	Ladram Bay camp-site	(0395) 68398
	Tourist Information, Sidmouth	(0395) 516441
	Old Farmhouse, Sidmouth	(0395) 512284
23	Mason's Arms, Branscombe	(029780) 300
	Portselda, Branscombe	(029780) 213
	Dolphin Hotel, Beer	(0297) 20068
	Youth Hostel, Beer	(0297) 20296
	Garlands Hotel, Seaton	(0297) 20958
24	Tourist Information, Seaton	(0297) 21660
	St. Margarets, Seaton	(0297) 20462
	Tors Hotel, Seaton	(0297) 20531
25	Hook Farm camp-site, Lyme Regis	(0297) 442801
26	Tourist Information, Lyme Regis	(0297) 442138
	Old Monmouth Hotel, Lyme Regis	(0297) 442456

3 PUBLIC TRANSPORT

Bus Services Bus services connect a number of places on the South Devon coast (see symbols on the maps). The majority of services are Monday–Friday only, with only a few routes operating on Saturdays and Sundays. Enquire at local Post Offices or phone:

For services in the area Plymouth–Torquay: Western National. Laira Bridge Road, Plymouth, tel: (0752) 664011.

For services in the area Torquay–Sidmouth: Devon General and others: Exeter Bus Station tel: (0392) 56231 or Torbay tel: (0803) 613226.

You will be told where you can get the current time-tables at all of these numbers.

Rail Services The following BR stations serve the South Devon Coast Path area: Plymouth, Torquay, Teignmouth, Dawlish, Dawlish Warren and Exmouth. In the summer the Dartmouth and Torbay Steam Railway connects Paignton BR with Kingswear (ferry to Dartmouth).

4 WALKING IN THE TORBAY AREA (Brixham, Paignton, Torquay)

In 1968 Torquay, Paignton and Brixham were amalgamated to form Devon's largest holiday resort, Torbay, extending for almost 20 miles of coast, with a resident population of over 120,000.

The official Coast Path from Brixham finishes temporarily after 2 miles at Goodrington (Paignton). On the other side of Torquay, from above the harbour, there are a number of cliff paths with fine views.

By changing buses at Torquay, you can travel from Goodrington to Babbacombe (Oddicombe). The bus runs via Paignton. If you prefer to walk as far as you can on paths without much road-walking here are the details.

From Fishcombe Road, Brixham, (Walk 14) take the Path which leads steeply down through woods towards the sea. After rather a scramble you will come out to the delightful Churston Cove. You climb out of Churston Cove by a steep narrow zig-zag path over the rocks which brings you, through woods, along the fence of the Churston Golf Course for about 1 mile (1½km). You then emerge from the woods above Elberry Cove. Walk along the beach, following the curve of Broad Sands Beach, mainly pebbles. The Path then turns inland to cross the Torbay Steam Railway (see Walk 13) and runs along the side of the line as far as Goodrington. Distance from Fishcombe Road: 2½ miles (4km).

East of Torquay there is a path just east of the harbour, above Peaked Tor Cove, which skirts Meadfoot Beach. Taking Marine Drive you come to the spectacular Hope's Nose by a path. Off the Nose are the islands, Thatcher's Rock, Ore Stone and Flat Rock, the last-named being the home of hundreds of gulls — it has the largest breeding colony of kittiwakes in Devon.

Rejoining Marine Drive a wooded path, Bishop's Walk, leads round Black Head and Anstey's Cove back to the road. A few yards along, a path runs round Long Quarry Point and down into Babbacombe Beach with its tiny pier. There is a good pub, the Fishermen's Arms. The Path continues just above beach level and starts climbing near the lower station of the Cliff Railway on Oddicombe beach.

The whole distance from the harbour is about 3½ miles (5½km).

Plymouth (pop. 243,000): famous city and naval port, previously known as Sutton Harbour. It was taken over in 1250 by the priors of Plympton and renamed Plymouth. At the mouth of two rivers, the Tamar and the Plym, with its magnificent anchorage, Plymouth Sound, it grew in importance as a military port. It was the home of Drake and Hawkins and the fleet sailed from here against the Armada.

It was in 1620 that the *Mayflower* sailed from Plymouth with 102 Pilgrim Fathers on their historic voyage to the New World and this event is commemorated here by a monument.

In the 17th century, fortifications and a naval dockyard were built. The next two centuries saw extensive growth but in August 1941 the centre of the city suffered immense destruction in air-raids. This has been rebuilt and Plymouth is now not only a thriving industrial city but also a major resort. There are 16th-century houses in New Street near Sutton Harbour and the old Barbican.

Locations: Bus Station — Breton Side (near Civic Centre); Head Post Office — St. Andrews Cross (near Civic Centre).

Torquay (pop. 54,000) before the 19th century was only a small Devon hamlet. The monks of Torre Abbey, founded in the 12th century, had been responsible for building the first small harbour where the present one stands. During the Napoleonic Wars (1796–1815) the British fleet spent much time anchored in Tor Bay and the officers, recognising the beauty and mild climate of Torquay, installed their wives and families there. Helped by the arrival of the railway in 1848, Torquay grew further and prospered.

Places of interest: *Kent's Cavern* (unique archaeological remains).

Torre Abbey Parts of the old abbey still remain, including the gatehouse, and the 16th-century house, set in pleasant gardens.

Cockington An old 16th-century village, preserved on the west outskirts of Torquay.

Torquay and Paignton (adjoining on the south) have 19 beaches to choose from. In Torquay, The Strand, just above the Inner Harbour, could be called the centre of the resort. Most local bus services start or call there.

Addresses in Torquay and Paignton:

Torquay Information Bureau, 9 Vaughan Parade (Inner Harbour) tel: (0803) 297428; General Post Office, Fleet Street (near The Strand); Police Station, South Street.

Paignton Information Bureau, The Esplanade tel: (0803) 558383; General Post Office, Palace Avenue.

5 WILDLIFE

The Coast Path passes through rich and varied habitats but many forms of wildlife need to be looked for carefully. Most mammals are retiring and nocturnal so you will be very lucky to see them but, to the observant, signs may be abundant.

Signs of badgers are very common though easily missed. Look out for groups of large holes a foot or more in diameter with substantial spoil heaps; distinct paths, forming a tunnel straight through dense vegetation. Soft mud may reveal their footprints, five-toed and with a broad heel, or those of a fox, very like a dog with four symmetrical toes, but more slender. The pungent odour of fox is often detected and if you are lucky you may occasionally see a fox or one of the smaller predators such as weasel or stoat.

The large freshwater lagoon known as Slapton Ley hosts a wealth of wildlife and it is well worth taking time to explore this beautiful nature reserve. Once a stronghold of otters, the Ley is still visited by this shy and elusive animal which might, if you are very lucky, be glimpsed from the bridge after dark. More common, though no less interesting, is the mink, like a small black cat with short legs and as much at home in the water as it is on the land.

Rabbits are now abundant and likely to become as serious a pest as they were forty years ago. Wherever there are rabbits you will find the vegetation nibbled close to the ground and liberally scattered with their droppings. Smaller mammals such as mice and voles are less likely to be seen although, if you listen closely while stopping for a break, you may hear them scurrying through the vegetation. Those with acute hearing may even hear the high pitched squeaks made by shrews.

Perhaps the most exciting mammals to look out for

are those living in the sea — whales, dolphins and seals. The grey seal population is somewhat scattered, but they can often be seen off rocky shores, particularly around Prawle Point and are well worth looking out for between Start Point and Bolt Tail. This is also the place from which to look for dolphins and whales. Although 12 species have been seen in south-western waters, most of these keep well out to sea and you are only likely to see bottle-nosed, or occasionally Risso's, dolphins inshore. However, common dolphins and, if you are extremely lucky, pilot whales or killer whales may occasionally come in close enough to be sighted from the cliff tops.

Turning back to the land and smaller forms of life, common lizards are indeed common, but you have to be quick to see them. Often a quick rustle at the side of the path will draw your attention to the sight of a slender tail vanishing into the undergrowth. Adders are also common and may be seen basking in the sun, particularly in the morning during spring or early summer.

Finally, we come to the insects. Butterflies are the most spectacular and in mid-summer will be seen in great numbers collecting energy-rich nectar from the coastal flowers. Early in the year, Brimstone and Orange-tip butterflies are amongst the first to be seen and the variety increases as summer progresses — Speckled Wood, Comma, Tortoiseshell, Peacock and Painted Lady are all abundant. Dragonflies and the smaller, delicate damselflies may be seen almost anywhere but are particularly varied at Slapton Ley. On a warm summer's day the buzz of bumblebees and the chirp of crickets and grasshoppers will accompany you as you walk.

6 GEOLOGY, FLOWERS, BIRDS

The coast east of Plymouth is composed of Devonian sandstones and shales which give way as you go east to earlier sandstones, limestones, clays and chalk, or a mixture of these. They range in age from 70 to 350 million years. The characteristic red cliffs and soil for some distance east of Torquay are a later iron-stained sandstone which was formed in desert conditions, giving it the 'burnt' appearance. Of particular interest on this sector are the landslip areas of which the one between Seaton and Lyme Regis is the best-known. This and other areas of geological, botanical and bird interest are mentioned below.

On the Path you come across what are known as raised beaches. Just east of Prawle Point and east of Teignmouth, for example, the beach has risen some feet and the sea-cliffs are now a little inland. One theory is that the beach level sprang back after being relieved of the weight of the ice of the Ice Age.

Beer Head The high chalk cliffs make a superb vantage point for bird-watching, particularly in the autumn: gannets off-shore, also kittiwakes, lesser black-backed gulls, shearwaters, terns, and the occasional skua; there are land migrations of wagtails, meadow pipits and tree pipits. Species that may be observed during autumn migration include chiffchaff, blackcap, willow warbler, spotted flychatcher, redstart, lesser whitethroat, ring ouzel, sedge warbler and pied flycatcher.

The vegetation is in strong contrast to that of the rest of the Devon coast. Gone is the heather, bracken and gorse which will by now be so familiar to the walker. It is replaced by short turf with shrubs such as wild privet, hawthorn and dogwood, with also wayfaring tree and scrambling old man's beard showing the presence of lime in the soil. Look out for mullion and nodding thistle.

Slapton Ley This is the largest freshwater area in the British Isles so close to the sea, covering 248 acres. Water is impounded by a shingle ridge and sixty per cent of the shingle is composed of flint. The Ley and the shingle ridge form part of a Nature Reserve. There are excellent shore and aquatic plants. The area is on the main line of coastal bird migration and the Ley attracts wintering fowl. A large coot population is found here and reed warblers are common.

Axmouth to Lyme Regis Undercliffs This landslip area is a Nature Reserve. Of great interest geologically, cliffs composed of chalk with sandstone and clays beneath have collapsed exposing fossil-bearing limestone and creating an unusual vegetation including an indigenous ash wood (see Walk 24).

Dawlish Warren Sand Dunes Flora includes the interesting maritime species zostera or eel grass, also fenugreek, soft and suffocating clover, chaffweed, flax seed, glassworth on the mud and two interesting grasses — giant quaking grass and harestail. Sand crocuses are also to be found. There is a Nature Reserve and a hide for watching birds in the estuary — a splendid spot.

INTRODUCTION TO DARTMOOR

Dartmoor is a vast oval with a bulge on the northeast side. There are three main topographical areas, the northern and southern fens (areas of peat blanket-bog) and the central basin (central oasis-depression drained by the River Dart and tributaries). The perimeter of the Moor is sharply defined by an escarpment of varying steepness. The overall dimensions are about 30 miles (48km) from north to south, and 17 miles (27km) from east to west.

Perhaps most characteristic of this great upland are the granite tors and their clitters — the extensive rockfields below the tors consisting of their debris; the huge depression of the central basin (most highland regions have a central *apex*); the swift and beautiful rivers and the gorges through which they leave the Moor; and the long, sweeping ridges. Notable, too, are the four medieval monasteries (one, Buckfast, revived today) around the south foot of the Moor, the innumerable remains of prehistoric occupation and burial monuments, and the highly unusual relics of medieval longhouses, most of them stricken by the Black Death of 1348.

Agriculture and industry, military training and other forms of development and land-use compete severely with conservation and recreational interests on a battle-ground of oscillating outcome. Even recreational demand is in itself so intense as literally to wear away the moor in places such as 'honey-pot' river banks and tors of easy access near the Moor's edge. To ensure the preservation of Dartmoor's terrain, it is important to observe conscientiously all notices and the Country Code. Please remember that it is an offence to feed the ponies. Remember, too, that many Devon lanes are deep, steep and narrow, and drivers venturing into them should be as competent to drive backwards as forwards!

An upland of such aloofness and so highly charged with atmosphere as Dartmoor, is inevitably rich in legendary lore, and has cradled crafts, place-names and customs kept alive to this day by an indigenous respect for tradition. These include such activities as building with granite, making 'scrumpy' (rough cider), riding the pony drifts (galloping at speed over the Moor to gather wild ponies) and sheep cattle herding on horseback, in which women of the moor take part alongside the men. The Dartmoor dialect, too, enshrines place-names based on Saxon and even Celtic roots.

Dartmoor's geological wealth: the thermal complexities governing the cooling of the granite created rich mineral veins. Tin occurs on the high moorland; iron and copper successively on the perimeter and in the border-country. Following a history covering many centuries, mining in the Dartmoor country ceased before World War II. Peat, formed by decaying vegetation, has also been cut, transported and marketed since the Middle Ages; as time went on its use became chiefly as industrial fuel and for the home hearth. China Clay, another substance resulting from the chemical change caused by decay - this time of the granite - is now a huge industry on the granite moors of Devon and Cornwall. Granite quarried from the heart of the tors was exported for almost two centuries until recent years, much of it going into some of London's most important buildings.

The Moor and its border-country formed one of England's first National Parks and was designated on 30 October 1951. The headquarters of the Park authority are at Parke, Bovey Tracey, Devon TQ13 9JQ; tel Bovey Tracey 832093 (open Mon–Fri 0900–1700). Dartmoor National Park Information Centres are at Princetown, Postbridge, Holne New Bridge, Steps Bridge (Teign Valley), Okehampton, Tavistock and Parke, Bovey Tracey.

1 WALKING SAFELY

It is advisable for walkers to wear well greased boots, woollen trousers and a brightly coloured outer garment which can be seen at a distance. Even in summer, an extra woollen garment and an anorak should be carried. Poised as it is on the South-West peninsula between two seas, Dartmoor experiences heavy rainfall with a high incidence of mist and strong winds. It is important not to underestimate the dangers of poor weather conditions, especially in the vicinity of a large mire. As Dartmoor rivers attain to flood particularly quickly, do not venture out to start a walk in torrential rain. Rivers in spate are exceedingly dangerous. If you are overtaken by mist when crossing a tract of open moor, do not go on but try to retrace your steps and return to the start. It is always sensible to tell someone where you are going before you set out. If any accidents do occur and it is possible for someone to reach a telephone, the Dartmoor Rescue Service can be summoned by dialling 999.

Water flowing over granite is self-purifying and is drinkable provided there are no houses nearby or dead animals lying in or near the water within 100 yards (91m). Any cuts can be cleaned effectively with sphagnum moss, which will prevent them from going septic.

Three military firing ranges on north Dartmoor are in use except in August. Times of firing are advertised in the *Western Morning News* and other local newspapers as well as in Post Offices, Police Stations and Dartmoor Information Centres. Red flags on tor and hill summits indicate that the range is in use. Red and white striped warning posts indicate the limit of safe approach to a range area in use and **must never be disregarded. Refrain from picking up any metal objects on or near a firing range.**

Although each route in this guide is mapped clearly, it is always worthwhile to take a detailed area map on any walk as this enables you to gain a wider view both for pleasure and safety.

Walking on Dartmoor is very time-consuming due to constant changes in terrain and due allowance should be made for this, as well as for undulations and strong winds, when calculating the probable time needed for a walk. Spot heights in metres are indicated on the maps. You should also consider the time taken to inspect historical features, which are far more numerous than in other British highland regions. As a general guide allow 35–45 minutes for each mile to be covered.

2 PUBLIC RIGHTS OF WAY

On Dartmoor public rights of way extend over open moorland, sometimes on recognisable paths and tracks but often over unmarked ground. They also exist where there is a notice announcing 'Footpath', 'Public Footpath' or 'Bridle Path'.

Permitted paths and access by traditional let exist through newtakes enclosed by broken walls or by maintained walls with unlocked gates. It should, however, be clear that much of the land is privately owned and some of the valley is enclosed.

Access to common land: the Forest of Dartmoor, the commons of Devon and a scatter of memorial commons (together covering 41% of the National Park), comprise most of the unenclosed land. The Dartmoor Commons Act, 1985, legalises public access to common land in the National Park and makes provision for byelaws to regulate public behaviour.

3 FLORA AND FAUNA

There is an abundance of delicate plant growth; rushes; grasses, mosses and lichens exist in many varieties. Three main types of heather appear — ling, bell-heather and cross-leaved heath. In late summer, blackberry and whortleberry, or blueberry, plants provide luscious fruit. The yellow heads of tormentil appear everywhere, ladies bedstraw can be found in dry soil and ivy-leafed bell flower grows in damp conditions.

Farm animals will normally be harmless but it is wise to keep a dog at heel in hot weather when flies may make cattle fractious and dogs must be strictly controlled and not allowed to run free at calving or lambing time. Bullocks will be harmless but if you enter illegally an enclosed and barred newtake you may come face-to-face with a Red Devon Bull which is large and uncertain of temper. If you encounter any ponies, remember that it is an offence to feed them. Grass snakes are harmless. If you see an adder, which is not harmless, with its distinctive zip-fastener marking, do not attack him but simply let him go. If you are alone and silent, a badger, otter or the occasional red fox may be glimpsed. You may see the buzzard, kestrel, sparrow-hawk, raven, wheatear, dipper or heron. The skylark is ubiquitous and the cuckoo calls amid the tors in May and June.

You may also encounter Scottish highland midgies, webless black spiders, black slugs, gorgeous dragonflies, honey bees (most hives are the property of Buckfast Abbey) and the striking green, black and orange caterpillar of the Emperor Moth.

4 GLOSSARY OF DARTMOOR TERMS

Adit horizontal tunnel driven by miners to drain a mine-working, or provide access to a vertical shaft.

Ancient Tenement a farm in the central basin established in Norman times, or earlier, with rights of turbary and pasture in return for stock-ranger duties performed for the lord of the soil.

Blowing house medieval workshop for processing tin-ore. The remains of some today contain relics of furnace, water-wheel pit, drop-stamps mortar stones and mould stones in which tin ingots were cast.

Bond-stone a boundary stone, sometimes unmarked, sometimes inscribed with initials of parish or land-owner.

Bronze Age period of pre-history *c* 1950–500 BC.

Bury artificial mound built for the colonising of rabbits on a warren.

Cleave valley with steep sides, a gorge.

Clitter scattered rockfield below a ruined tor, ice-transported during the Ice Age.

Combe a valley closed at one end.

Cornditch ditch dug on outer side of enclosure wall, the earth being thrown behind the wall to create a bank. Thus deer could not jump into the enclosure but any that entered through an open gate could leap outwards. In short, a ditch to protect the corn.

Cross, granite, medieval rough-hewn from solid granite by monks and erected by them to function as Christian way-marks.

Dolmen Neolithic (*ie* pre-Bronze Age) burial chamber built with large stone uprights and a slab roof.

Featherbed (i) see 'Granite Bedding'; (ii) a mire that undulates when trodden on.

Fen the peat bog areas of north and south Dartmoor.

Field system a prehistoric field-plan marked out by reaves.

Gert a deep cutting made by miners to reach a vein of tin.

Granite bedding a solid granite platform, often found on tor summits and in river beds.

Gulf see 'Gert'

Hole a small gorge.

Hut circle circular stone remains of prehistoric dwelling, originally thatched.

Iron Age period of pre-history *c* 500BC–50AD.

Kistvaen a stone chest for burial of human remains in the Bronze Age, usually by cremation.

Lake a tributary stream of which the source, drained by tinners, was once a tarn.

Leat artificial channel contouring hillsides to carry water by gravity.

Logan stone a rock pivoted upon another at a fine point of balance caused by weathering, and capable of being rocked.

Longhouse traditional Devon farmhouse with central passage dividing human from animal quarters. Many medieval longhouse ruins remain on Dartmoor, most emptied by the Black Death in 1348.

Menhir Celtic - a tall stone; prehistoric monument usually associated with burial.

Mire a valley swamp

Moorgate access gate to open moor at head of border-country lane.

Mortar stone see 'Blowing house'.

Newtake land taken in from open moorland

Pound enclosure for animals, usually circular.

Reave a boundary bank of earth and stone; some are prehistoric, some medieval.

Retaining circle of small set stones surrounding a Bronze Age interment.

Rock basin natural hollow produced on tors by weathering, and in rivers by erosion.

Slotted gateposts granite posts slotted to receive lateral poles, precursor of the hinged gate.

Stannary (Latin *Stanum* - Tin) the highly organised medieval tin industry on Dartmoor.

Stone circle open-air temple of the Bronze Age.

Stone row monumental row of set stones leading from a Bronze Age interment to a terminal stone. The longest known in the world, two and a half miles (4km) in length, is in the Erme valley on southern Dartmoor.

Tare and feather method of cutting granite after *c* 1800 by inserting punches (tares) into pre-drilled holes, kept in position by tiny iron blades (feathers) and hammering on the tares.

Tinner a medieval worker in tin.

Tinners' house medieval tinners' work-a-week shelter: a tiny house with wolf-proof cupboard and fireplace.

Tor (also Rock) Celtic *Twr,* Cornish *Tour* a rockpile; most have been ruined by Ice Age conditions and weathered in vertical partings and horizontal jointings.

Vermin trap, granite miniature granite tunnel, built and sited by warreners to protect buries from predators. The tunnel had a false floor which, when trodden on, released slate shutters imprisoning the animal.

Warren a rabbit farm; some are of medieval foundation, Ditsworthy and Trowlesworthy on southern Dartmoor being the oldest. Sporting warrens were established by landowners for sport and for replenishing their larders.

Waste a term peculiar to south Dartmoor. It indicates a former open tract of moorland, later enclosed.

Walk 1 — Coastal Path
WEMBURY (PLYMOUTH)– GARA POINT

7 miles (11¼km); easy
Cum. 10¾miles (17 km)

The South Devon Coast Path starts at Turnchapel on Plymouth Sound and the cumulative distance given is from this point. Initially this involves some road-walking through built-up areas. We, therefore, recommend that in the summer months you start at Wembury Beach (No. 48 bus from Plymouth) or at Heybrook Bay (No. 49 bus). Even then, you are limited by the River Yealm ferry which runs only in July and August (see below). From September to June you can start from Newton Ferrers or Noss Mayo (No. 94 bus). Note there is no service on these three lines on Sundays and Bank Holidays.

From Wembury Beach to Newton Ferrers, an attractive sailing centre, the going is fine; open cliff-top country, mainly pasture. Newton Ferrers is joined by the road encircling the inlet to Noss Mayo, another hamlet.

Wembury has a 15th-century church with a 14th-century tower, a prominent landmark for mariners. There is a pleasant sandy beach and up the road from the beach is the Old Wheel pub. Newton Ferrers church is predominantly 15th-century with 13th-century parts. The nearest pubs are the Dolphin at Newton Ferrers, the Swan and the Old Ship at Noss Mayo.

The Yealm ferry runs in July and August, up to 7pm in good weather, to Newton Ferrers and Noss Mayo or directly across to the Coast Path. When on the west bank shout for attention. However, it is advisable to phone the operators beforehand . Tel: (0752) 072189.

The road becomes a wide Path, climbing past former Coast Guard cottages to Gara Point, with fine views along the coast.

Note that after Newton Ferrers there are no refreshments for 15 miles (24km), except for a small shop at Stoke (summer only).

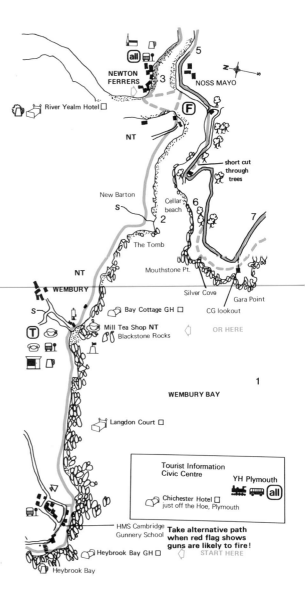

14

Walk 2 — Coastal Path
GARA POINT–BEACON HILL
4 miles (6½km); easy
Cum. 14¾ miles (23¾km)

On the next section, Beacon Hill – Beacon Point, you have to cross the Erme Estuary. There is no bridge or ferry so the only method is to wade across and this is only possible at low tide. You will need to take this into consideration when planning your walk. Hints on how to find the time of high and low tide are given on pages 6–7.

The Path continues as a wide track round Gara Point, along the 200-foot (60m) cliff top with wide sea views and past the lone Warren Cottage. Seals and porpoises may be seen in the summer. The countryside inland is quite unspoiled and empty of human habitation except for a farmhouse or two. After rounding Stoke Point, the Path passes through a pleasing patch of woodland, coming out at a road junction and a small cluster of houses around Stoke House.

Approaching Stoke Point, a diversion can be made on the seaward side by following a footpath to the 14th-century St. Peter's Church, the abandoned former parish church of Noss Mayo, nearly 2 miles (3¼km) from the village. Here is another ancient church which could very well have been built to provide a visual guide to shipping. Look for the tombstone, reputed to be that of a pirate, on the floor in the south-east corner. Look, also, for the tablet to Miriam K. Kingscombe.

The Path can be regained by a steep road through a caravan site. There is a store at the site with refreshments in the summer.

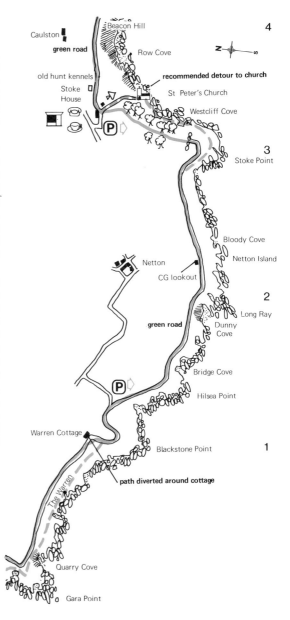

Walk 3 — Coastal Path

BEACON HILL–
BEACON POINT

4¾ miles (7¾km); strenuous

Cum. 19½ miles (31½km)

From Beacon Hill the track of the Path is clear and continues along the cliff top, with one or two quite steep slopes to negotiate, including St. Anchorite's Rock and Bugle Hole. Watch for the warning on the map avoiding a tendency to veer landward. The Path then turns inland above the shore of the River Erme affording fine views of Bigbury Bay and beyond and descends to the pleasant Mothecombe Beach.

The river must be forded. It should be possible to wade across for about an hour each side of low tide (see pages 6–7 for a guide on how to find out the approximate times of high and low tide). You can make directly across towards Wonwell Beach with the ruined cottages — one was a pilot house, painted white as a navigation mark for shipping. **Check locally that it is safe to cross. The ford can be dangerous after heavy rains.**

From the beach the Path climbs clearly, bordering agricultural land, following the cliff edge, until the 300-foot (90m) Beacon Point is rounded.

As an alternative to wading the Erme or if the tide is not low enough you can walk, mainly on country roads, via Holbeton (2 miles/3¼km), Hole Farm and Sequer's Bridge (taking the A379 across the river) and Kingston. To rejoin the Path the total distance of the diversion is 7 miles (11¼km). Holbeton has a good pub and accommodation.

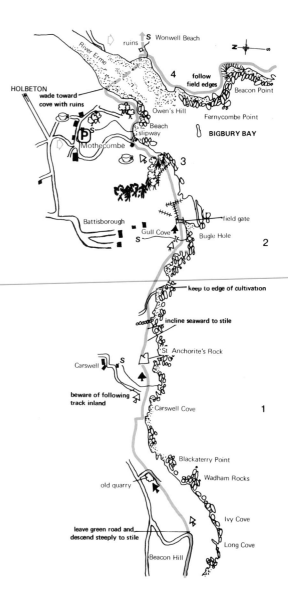

Walk 4 — Coastal Path
BEACON POINT–
BIGBURY ON SEA
3¾ miles (6km); strenuous
Cum. 23¼ miles (37½km)

From Beacon Point for 2 miles (3¼km) the Path runs as a narrow track between the boundary fence of the Scabbiscombe estate and the cliff edge — very close in some places. There are some extremely steep gradients, particularly that leading down to Westcombe Beach and up the other side, and these need careful negotiation especially in wet or windy weather.

At Ringmore, 1 mile (1½km) inland, is the Journey's End Inn, where Sheriff wrote his famous play of World War I. Accommodation is available. The village itself is of interest with its 13th-century church.

Challaborough has a sandy beach but bathing can be dangerous at certain times. Bigbury on Sea, a bungalow resort, crowded in summer, offers all the usual facilities. Off Bigbury and connected by a 300-yard (275m) sandy causeway is Burgh Island. The only buildings are the large hotel and the Pilchard pub, dating from the mid-14th century. The hotel, home in the 1930's of a millionaire, has been carefully restored in the period style. At high tide a tractor on stilts (designed by a visitor) takes you across.

You now have to cross the River Avon or Aune (pronounced 'Orne') from Bigbury to Bantham. The ferry runs for two weeks at Easter and from mid-May to the end of August, Mon–Sat 10am–11am and 3pm–4pm. The ferry is operated from Bantham opposite, tel: (0548) 560593. The best route to the ferry point, except at high tide, is along the sands. At high tide, walk along the busy main road (see also next map) for about 1 mile (1½km), turning off down the footpath alongside Mount Folly Farm. See Walk 5 for an inland alternative to the ferry.

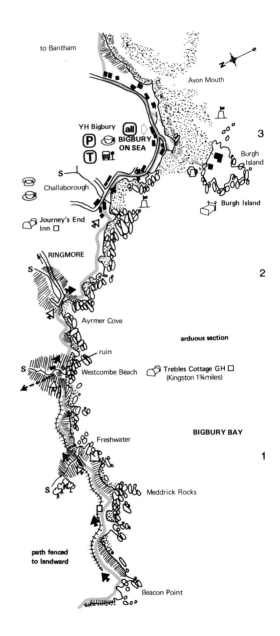

Walk 5 — Coastal Path

BANTHAM–THURLESTONE–
HOPE–BOLT TAIL

4¾ miles (7¾km); moderate
Cum. 28 miles (45¼km)

As an alternative to the Avon ferry you can walk by country road and footpath inland via Aveton Gifford (with the aid of a local map), about 7 miles (11¼km). Alternatively, take a taxi, tel: (0548) 856120. The distance is about 9 miles (14½km) to Bantham.

At Bantham, the medieval Sloop Inn provides accommodation.

The sandhills and the sandy shore at Bantham attract many motorists and their families in the summer. The Path runs parallel to the bank of the estuary and then turns south-east to follow the coast, running along the seaward boundary of the Thurlestone Golf Course for 1¾ miles (2½km).

Thurlestone (derived from Old English meaning 'pierced stone' from the arched rock on the shore) is another holiday resort with excellent sands and safe bathing. The old village is 1 mile (1½km) inland.

As there are houses right up to the edge of the cliff the Path follows the road inland for a short way and then turns to the right and climbs along the cliff. You soon arrive above the much-photographed twin villages of Inner and Outer Hope, the old part huddled round the sandy Hope Cove. In the high season there is much congestion with cars, coaches and crowds. A quiet and beautiful spot is the Square in Inner Hope, just behind the street above the cove.

The Path climbs quite steeply from the road in Inner Hope by the old Methodist chapel to the impressive headland, Bolt Tail, with the clear imprint of an Iron Age cliff fort on the summit.

It was off Bolt Tail that disaster overtook *HMS Ramilles* in the winter of 1760 when she was wrecked with the loss of 800 crew and passengers. There were only a few survivors.

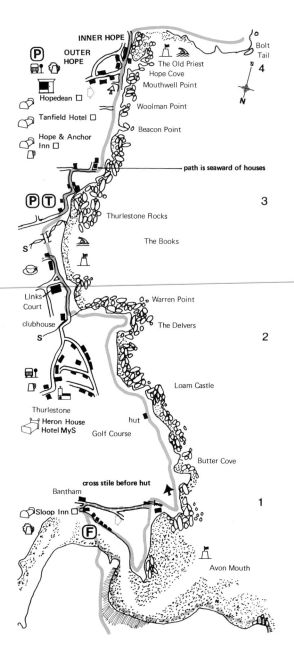

Walk 6 — Coastal Path

BOLT TAIL–THE WARREN

3¼ miles (5¼km); strenuous

Cum. 31¼ miles (50¼km)

From Bolt Tail for 5 miles (8km) to Bolt Head the Path follows the coastline high above the sea providing probably the most spectacular high cliff-walking on the south coast. Some steep gradients are to be overcome.

The massive rock formations for 10 miles (16km) from Bolt Tail to Prawle Point and for a few miles inland are very distinctive to this stretch of the coast. Known as metamorphosed mica schists, the original rocks have been transformed through gigantic geological pressures. The shining flakes of mica and white outcrops of quartz may be seen. Near the tall radio masts ahead on Bolberry Down (named after the nearby hamlet which is mentioned in the Domesday Book) is a road, serving a former wartime installation, which brings motorists to view the cliffs in the summer. There are refreshment facilities during the season at the Port Light, by the radio masts.

The going becomes steep on the sharp descent to Soar Mill Cove, with an equally exacting gradient up the other side. There are one or two paths to choose from but it can be a steep slope whichever you choose.

The whole area from just the other side of Bolt Tail to Bolt Head is National Trust land. In their pamphlet, they draw attention to the birds and wild flowers. Besides herring and greater black-backed gulls there are shags and fulmars to be seen on the cliffs in the early summer. There are also ravens, buzzards and stonechats. Among the wild flowers, you can find the delicate blue vernal squill.

Once past Soar Mill Cove the Path to Bolt Head via the Warren presents no difficulty.

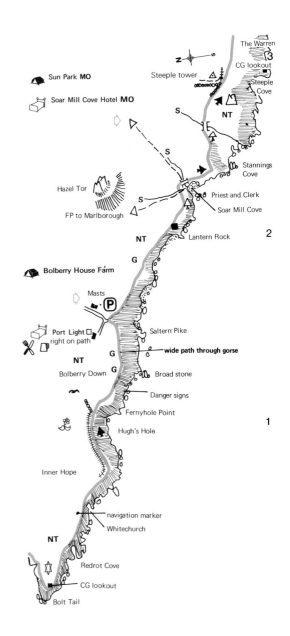

Walk 7 — Coastal Path
THE WARREN–BOLT HEAD–SALCOMBE–GARA ROCK
5¾ miles (9¼km); strenuous
Cum. 37 miles (59½km)

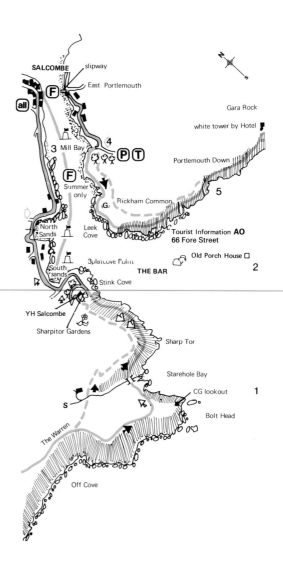

Beyond the Warren more than one path leads to Salcombe but the most attractive is along the cliff edge following the sign 'South Sands via Bolt Head' up to the Head, down to Starehole Bay until joining the paved Courtney Walk. Sharp left at the end of the Walk is Sharpitor Gardens (museum) and the youth hostel. Rounding the 400-foot (120m) Sharp Tor you have a fine view of Salcombe and the estuary. The road leads down to South Sands and North Sands beaches. There is a ferry from South Sands to the centre of Salcombe in the summer.

Salcombe (pop. 2500), Devon's most southerly resort, is probably the largest yachting centre in Britain, the estuary and its branches providing superb anchorage. Fishing is also popular. Fore Street has some delightful buildings and there is the ruined Salcombe Castle, or Fort Charles, which was built by Henry VIII.

The ferry runs from Fore Street to East Portlemouth (for the Coast Path). Last departure Apr–Oct: 7.30pm, Nov–Mar: 5.00pm.

The attractive village of East Portlemouth rivalled Salcombe in the Middle Ages, sending five ships for Henry V's invasion fleet.

The road from the ferry leads to the small safe sandy beaches of Small's Cove and Mill Bay. From Mill Bay the Coast Path continues alongside the estuary shore, through woods and follows the cliff edge up to the slopes below the prominent Gara Rock with its flagstaff.

Note: unless you make the detour inland to East Prawle (see Walk 8) there are no refreshment facilities in the 10 miles (16km) between Gara Rock and the Hallsands.

20

Walk 8 — Coastal Path

GARA ROCK–PRAWLE POINT– LANNACOMBE BAY

4¼ miles (6¾km); strenuous
Cum. 41¼ miles (66½km)

Although almost as spectacular as the Bolt Tail to Bolt Head stretch, this part of the Path is more lonely and wild — mainly because road access is limited — with steep gradients as far as Prawle Point.

From below the Gara Rock Hotel the Path skirts above a small beach (there is also a path up to the hotel) and through National Trust land and along Deckler's Cliff to the precipitous Gammon Head, looking down at the two lonely, tempting beaches in Maceley Cove — reached by a steep path. If in need of refreshment you can take a track to East Prawle (1¼ miles/2km), rejoining by other tracks to Prawle Point or farther up the coast to Horseley Cove. Continue from Gammon Head past the Coast Guard lookout to Prawle Point.

Prawle Point is an excellent place for viewing migrating birds (particularly in the autumn) such as warblers and wheatears; for waders: turnstones, curlews, whimbrels, oystercatchers; and sea birds: terns, kittiwakes and shearwaters.

Once round the Point the scenery changes dramatically. Stretching in front of you is a 'shelf' of pasture and crops. You have here a fine view of the geologist's 'raised beach'. The 'shelf' was part of the sea bed; the original line of the cliffs, complete with caves, of up to 300 feet (275m) in height, can be seen approximately ½ mile (¾km) inland.

The Path from Prawle Point proceeds in front of the Coast Guard cottages and then along the seaward edge of the fields, along the edge of the low cliff, turning slightly inland opposite Ballsaddle Rock.

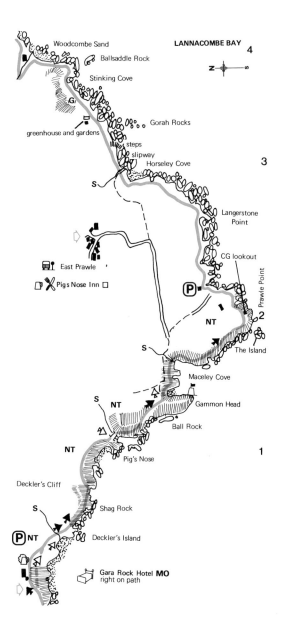

Walk 9 — Coastal Path
LANNACOMBE BAY–
START POINT–HALLSANDS
3½ miles (5½km); easy
Cum. 44¾ miles (72km)

The Path from Prawle Point leads above the small but pleasant Lannacombe Beach, which is sand and rock but good for swimming. The capacity of the very small car park protects the beach from overcrowding. From Lannacombe Beach the Path keeps to the coast, skirting Mattiscombe Beach **(swimming can be dangerous)** *on the way to Peartree Point and Start Point. Nearing the Point you have to climb to the top of the ridge which ends in the Point. You then come out on the road leading to the lighthouse and have a fine view of the next 15 miles (24¼km). Prominent in the northerly direction is Slapton Ley, the largest stretch of inland fresh water in Devon, bounded by Slapton Sands, a 5-mile (8km) barrier of shingle and sand.*

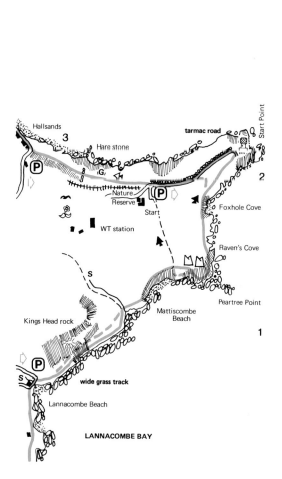

Start Point Lighthouse was built in 1836; 'start' means 'tail' in Anglo-Saxon (compare 'redstart', the bird) and the rocky 'tail' of the Point has been the gravestone of many ships. The lighthouse may be visited every afternoon from Monday to Saturday. Start Point is a nature reserve and in spring and autumn is a good spot for viewing migrating birds.

The route of the Path follows the lighthouse road inland for about ½ mile (¾km) and, at the car park, turns off along the cliff top through gorse and bracken. Follow the waymark down into Hallsands.

At the end of the 19th century, a quantity of shingle was removed from the beach at Hallsands for construction work in Plymouth docks. This weakened the defences and, after a storm in 1917, the houses on the seaward side of the main street were undermined and eventually collapsed. There are pictures of the tragedy in the local pubs.

Walk 10 — Coastal Path

HALLSANDS–TORCROSS–SLAPTON LEY

3½ miles (5½km); easy
Cum. 48¼ miles (77¾km)

The Path gives good easy walking along the cliff or the beach as far as Torcross. From Torcross, however, it is uncomfortably wedged between the main road and the edge of Slapton Ley and then for a short distance beyond Strete Gate (see Walk 11). The view of the waterfowl on the Ley could compensate for your discomfort. Beyond Strete Gate is road-walking all the way to Redlap past Stoke Fleming (Walk 12), a distance of 4 miles (6½km). To avoid road-walking there is a regular bus service from Torcross to Stoke Fleming (and to Dartmouth) except on Sundays and Bank Holidays.

Beesands is a small fishing village with a line of cottages overlooking the sea and was a victim of a German air raid in 1943. There is a good pub, the Cricket, and on the north side a large unattractive caravan site. Torcross, formerly a fishing hamlet but now catering for the holiday-maker provides all facilities, including an old pub, the Start Bay.

Slapton Ley, 2 miles long (3¼km) and covering 250 acres (100 hectares) is an important nature reserve. There is a bird-watching post of the Devon Bird-Watching and Preservation Society. In the village of Slapton ¾ mile (1¼km) inland, is the Slapton Ley Field Study Centre which controls entry to the reserve. The multitude of water plants in this shallow stretch of water attracts an abundance of insects — 17 species of dragon-fly, for example — much appreciated by birds arriving in the spring: warblers, martins and wagtails, also by wintering flocks of ducks: mallard, pochard and tufted duck. The marshes of the Higher Ley are a breeding place for reed warblers; sedge warblers are frequent visitors.

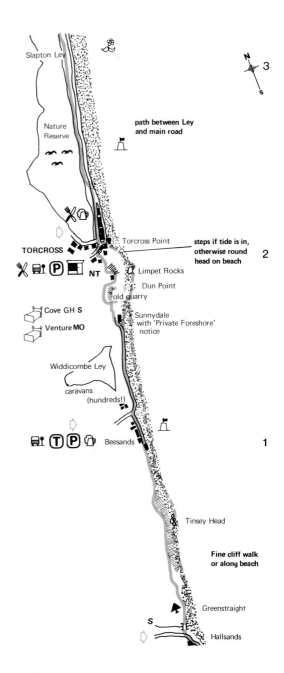

Walk 11 — Coastal Path
SLAPTON LEY–
BLACKPOOL SANDS
3½ miles (5½km); easy
Cum. 51¾ miles (83¼km)

The Path continues tediously alongside the main road and the edge of Slapton Ley and then to Strete Gate. From here you have to walk on the road itself through Strete and Blackpool Sands.

Slapton Beach was used by the Americans for rehearsal exercises for the Normandy landings. As live ammunition was used, hundreds of families had to be evacuated. The monument halfway along the beach commemorates these events.

You can break your journey at the villages of Slapton and Strete — both are of interest.

Slapton has a ruined 14th-century chantry which is mentioned in the Domesday Book, and two pubs: the Queens Arms and the Tower Inn. In Strete there is a ruined Edwardian manor house used as a picnic site and the King's Arms pub. Blackpool Sands is pleasant out of season but becomes crowded in the summer. It was the object of another invasion in 1304 when raiders from Brittany landed there, to be repulsed by the men of Dartmouth.

There are regular bus services along the main road except on Sundays and Bank Holidays if you wish to avoid road-walking.

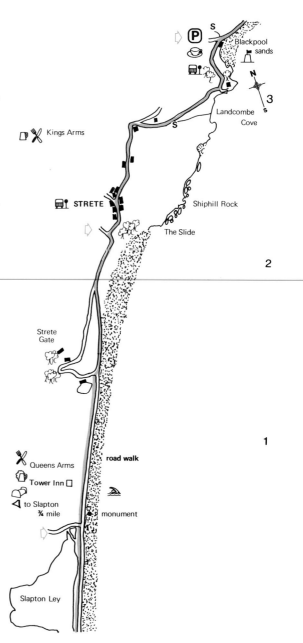

Walk 12 — Coastal Path
BLACKPOOL SANDS–
MILL BAY COVE
5¾ miles (9¼km); moderate
Cum. 57½ miles (92½km)

Still more road-walking along the main road until just past Stoke Fleming, a village with an impressive church with 14th-century brasses. Keep on, then turn right down a secondary road at some playing fields (if on a bus ask to be let off at Windward Corner). The road twists and turns through quiet pastureland reaching Redlap hamlet. Here is a car park and the western boundary of Little Dartmouth Cliff, a fine stretch 1½ miles (2½km) long of National Trust land. It was a gift from the Devon Women's Institute.

A sign directs the Path towards the coastline at Warren Cove before turning east along the high cliff top.

The name 'Warren' occurs frequently in this area. It refers to the hunting of rabbits, an important source of food in the past.

You continue along the gorse-and-bracken-covered cliff before you descend to Compass Cove — a little shingle beach with good swimming. Turn round Blackstone Point to the road and the 15th-century Dartmouth Castle on the outskirts of Dartmouth itself.

Dartmouth (pop. 6700), in its beautiful setting above the River Dart was an important sea port by the 12th century. It had busy trade links with the continent and was a departure point for the Crusades. The famous Royal Navy College dominates the hillside above the town. The two churches are worth a visit and there are some fine old houses and pubs near the waterfront.

The ferry to Kingswear runs daily throughout the year.

Take the street in Kingswear running parallel to the estuary and up Alma Steps. The Coast Path continues as a country road high above Mill Bay.

There is a daily steam railway from Kingswear to Paignton in the summer.

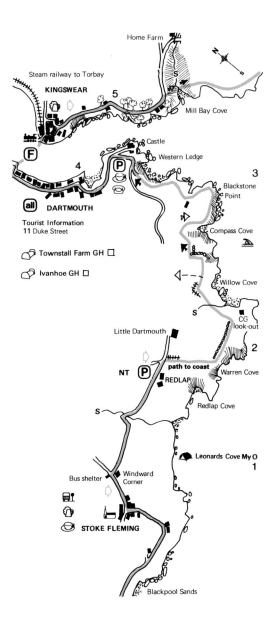

Walk 13 — Coastal Path
MILL BAY COVE–
MAN SANDS
4½ miles (7¼km); strenuous
Cum. 62 miles (99¾km)

Most of this stretch of the Coast Path lies in National Trust land. It is designated as an Area of Outstanding Natural Beauty and the scene delights at every turn.

As the road from Kingswear starts to curve inland, a Coast Path sign on the right directs you to a steep track down the green valley.

This valley and the woods above are known as The Warren and were a gift in 1984 to the nation in memory of Lieutenant Colonel Jones VC who died in the Falklands conflict. The small castle-like building in the valley was previously a mill.

On the headland, Inner Froward Point, you pass by what was a World War II gun battery and ¼ mile (400m) along a path inland is Day Beacon, built in 1864 as a navigation aid for shipping. The Path continues along the cliffs, dropping down to a series of small coves leading to Scabbacombe Sands.

The islet off Outer Froward Point is the Mew Stone, a nesting place of many sea-birds as are Scabbacombe Cliffs. Kittiwakes and graceful fulmars are among those to be seen. You are asked not to disturb nesting birds from March to June.

The National Trust draws attention to Pudcombe Coves where, at low tide, a wealth of marine life is exposed such as shellfish and sea-plants.

A further fine expanse of cliff-walking brings you to Crabrock Point, Man Sands and the former Coast Guard cottages. From Man Sands you are faced with a steep climb to the top of Southdown Cliff.

You can swim at Scabbacombe Sands and Man Sands.

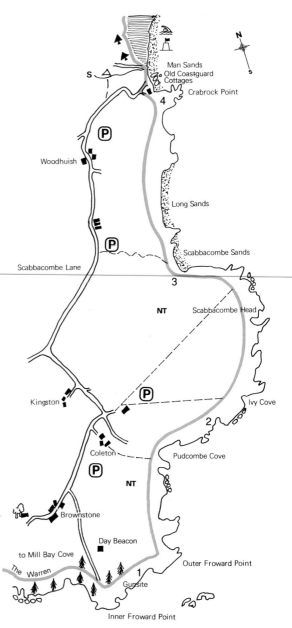

Walk 14 — Coastal Path

MAN SANDS–BRIXHAM

5 miles (8km); easy

Cum. 67 miles (107¾km)

The Path continues along Southdown Cliff, over springy turf. You come to Sharkham Point and then down to St. Mary's Bay.

St. Mary's Bay has a good beach of pebble and sand.

Climbing through thick undergrowth, the Path hugs the cliff edge round Durl Head. Next comes Berry Head Common and at the tip of the Head, the lighthouse.

Berry Head has been declared a Country Park. There is a nature trail and in the spring and early summer the cliffs are the breeding place of fulmars, kittiwakes and razorbills. There are traces of an Iron-Age cliff fort and massive remains of fortifications, a bulwark against Napoleonic forces.

The Path proceeds easily to Brixham.

Brixham has been a busy fishing port for centuries and the harbour preserves much of its earlier character. There is a statue of William of Orange who landed in Brixham in 1688 and who was to become King William III.

If you wish to pass through the town, catch a No. 17 bus from Berry Head Road (leading from the base of the Head) to the bus station, near the harbour and then a No. 118 bus to Fishcombe Road where you can join the Path again on the other side of the town. The No. 17 bus does not run on Sundays. The walk to the bus station is 1½ miles (2½km).

For notes on walking from Fishcombe Road to Goodrington (where the Path ends temporarily) and from the harbour in Torquay (where it resumes) to the beginning of Walk 15, see 'Walking in the Torbay area (Brixham, Paignton, Torquay)' on page 8.

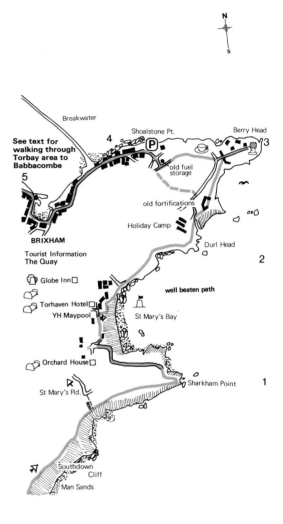

Walk 15 — Coastal Path
ODDICOMBE (TORQUAY)–
LABRADOR BAY
From Peaked Tor Cove:
7½ miles (12km); moderate
Cum. 74½ miles (119¾km)

The Coast Path leaves Oddicombe Beach near the lower station of the cliff railway and continues with a pleasant walk beside the beach. Starting with a climb above Petit Tor beach it enters a patch of thick woodland, emerging at Watcombe Beach in a completely wooded setting. A steep climb out of Watcombe, helped by some steps — with fine glimpses of the sea from the cliff top, through the trees — brings you eventually to the delightful village of Maidencombe.

Maidencombe has a sandy beach and the Thatched House pub which is open during the holiday season. The thatched cottages of the village seem unspoiled — although, because of the beach, there may be a flood of visitors in July and August.

From Maidencombe the route is along a field path close to the cliff edge which is obscured for most of the way by the undergrowth and trees bordering the Path on the seaward side. For the 1½ miles (2½km) from Maidencombe to where the Path comes out on the road (see Walk 16) you pass through undulating fields and woods, with the combes running to the sea. With no human habitation in sight the area is ideal for picnics.

For those walking towards the west, see the notes under 'Walking the Torbay area (Brixham, Paignton, Torquay)' on page 8 for how to rejoin the Coast Path at Brixham.

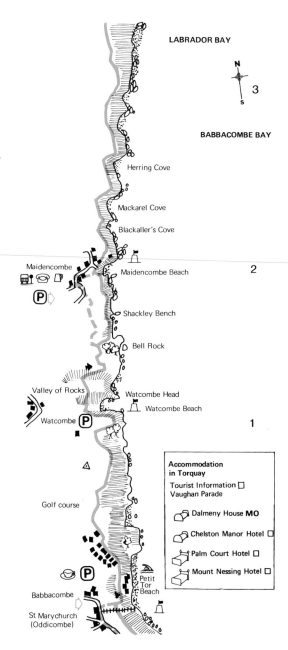

LABRADOR BAY

BABBACOMBE BAY

Herring Cove

Mackarel Cove

Blackaller's Cove

Maidencombe

Maidencombe Beach

Shackley Bench

Bell Rock

Valley of Rocks

Watcombe Head

Watcombe Beach

Watcombe

Golf course

Petit Tor Beach

Babbacombe

St Marychurch (Oddicombe)

Accommodation in Torquay

Tourist Information □
Vaughan Parade

Dalmeny House **MO**

Chelston Manor Hotel □

Palm Court Hotel □

Mount Nessing Hotel □

Walk 16 — Coastal Path
LABRADOR–
TEIGNMOUTH–HOLCOMBE
4 miles (6½km); moderate
Cum. 78½ miles (126¼km)

Leaving Labrador Bay the Path is diverted inland up a slope to the main A379 road for ¼ mile (400m). On the right there is a sign showing the Coast Path continuing across fields and along the cliff, round the Ness, to Shaldon.

There is a bridge over the Teign ½ mile (¾km) up the river from Shaldon to Teignmouth. Alternatively, the ferry leaves the foreshore on Marine Parade daily except November to Easter when it sails weekdays only. The last departure from mid-July to August is 10pm; other times 5pm; an hour or two later in early summer.

Teignmouth (pop. 13,000) can boast one of the earliest historical records of the South Coast; its seal dates back to Ethelred the Unready (AD1002). A port of some importance for 1000 years, the present major export is ball clay. Teignmouth was a victim of French raids in the 14th and 17th centuries and a target of many hit-and-run air-raids in World War II. With its fine sandy beach, it has long been considered an attractive resort.

The Coast Path route follows the promenade with the sea on one side and the railway on the other. Just where the line enters a tunnel you pass underneath and up Smugglers Lane to the main road at Holcombe.

The rock pillar off the shore is the Parson and Clerk.

If the tide is very high and the promenade unusable, for an alternative route, cross the footbridge near the station where the railway starts along the sea. This leads to a footpath over open ground bringing you to the main road, ½ mile (¾km) from Holcombe.

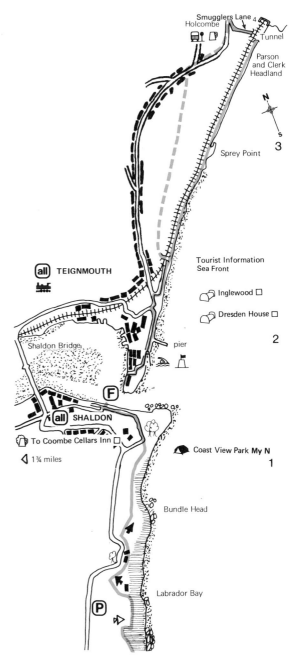

Walk 17 — Coastal Path

HOLCOMBE–DAWLISH–
DAWLISH WARREN

3½ miles (5½km); easy

Cum. 82 miles (132km)

Dawlish is a small fishing village that has
developed into a sizeable resort and residential
centre. The railway stimulated its growth as
the streets of Victorian villas testify.

   *When emerging from Smugglers Lane at
Holcombe follow the main road for 125 yards
(115m) then turn right. A Coast Path sign directs
you down Derncleugh Gardens. After a few steps
turn left along Windward Lane. A stile on the left
leads to the cliff edge. The route proceeds with fine
views and then turns left again. You walk on the
right down the quiet Old Teignmouth Road which
brings you to the main road which you follow for
about 25 yards (23m). Walk through a park on
the right to the promenade alongside the railway.*

   *If it is not high tide you can continue all the way
to the footbridge over the line just beyond Langstone
Rock to Dawlish Warren station.*

   *If the tide is up, join the main road from the park
mentioned above, on the town side of the railway.
Where this turns inland, on the right there is
Warren Road. You will see the Path on the right
running up to the cliff. This is the official Path but
the view is obstructed by high hedges. These
hedges, however, provide the Path with shelter from
the high tides and wind and rain coming off the sea.
Both routes go through to Dawlish Warren station,
and, stretching out into the estuary of the River
Exe, Dawlish Warren itself.*

   *In the routes given above you have to follow the
main road a couple of times when approaching
Dawlish. This is a busy road (A379) particularly
in summer. There is no pavement on this stretch on
the seaward side. Try not to walk on the road itself
and take good care when you cross the road.*

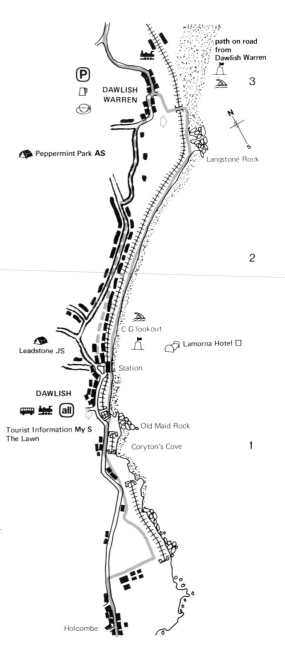

Walk 18 — Coastal Path
DAWLISH WARREN–
STARCROSS–EXMOUTH

3½ miles (5½km); easy
Cum. 85½ miles (137½km)

Dawlish Warren is a huge sand spit 1½ miles (2½km) long. It encloses a golf course, a nature reserve and, as is apparent from the road, a large caravan park. The reserve is of interest for its salt-water flora and, in particular, migrant birds.

From Dawlish Warren to Starcross you walk or take a bus along the road. You pass Cockwood (pronounced Co'wood) which has an old pub, the Anchor, to minister to your needs.

To continue you have to cross the River Exe so make allowance for this extra distance. There is a daily hourly ferry service from Starcross to Exmouth from 1 May to October. The last ferry from Starcross is at 6.30pm; from Exmouth 5.45pm.

When the ferry is not running you have to make a 20-mile (32¼km) detour via Exeter either by bus or train (infrequent). Allow at least 1½hrs.

The small village of Starcross has a unique distinction: its sailing club is the oldest in Britain — perhaps in the world — founded in the 18th century. Its four pubs, one 400 years old, complete the picture. One pub, the Atmospheric, recalls one of the few failures of the 19th-century engineer I K Brunel. This was an Atmospheric Railway from Exeter to Plymouth, the waggons being propelled by a piston running a vacuum pipe between the rails. A former pumping station for Brunel's line is now a museum in the village.

Exmouth (pop. 29,000) has been a resort since the 18th century when families from Exeter were attracted to its sandy beach. Lady Nelson and Lady Byron lived in the Georgian street, Beacon Hill.

In Exmouth the Path at first goes along the promenade. A road bears inland behind the car park and, a short way on the right, the Path takes to the cliffs. You can also continue to the end of the promenade and take the path that leads up to the cliff Path.

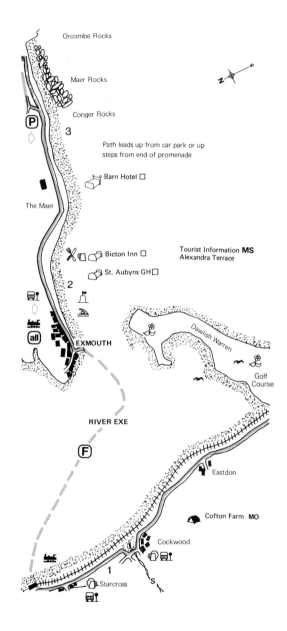

Walk 19 — Coastal Path

EXMOUTH–
BUDLEIGH SALTERTON

3½ miles (5½km); strenuous
Cum. 89 miles (143¼km)

From Orcombe Point, the Coast Path traverses National Trust land rising up the crest of the High Land of Orcombe Cliff (250 feet/75m) then descends to Sandy Bay and a large holiday park. A firing range occupies the headland of Straight Point so you must keep close to the wire fence bordering the holiday park on the descent to Littleham Cove.

The beaches of shingle and sand at Sandy Bay and Littleham are very popular in the season.

From the cliff above Littleham Cove you can see the route of the Path making its way gradually up to West Down Beacon, over 400 feet (120m) high, with splendid views.

Between the cliff and the sea is a wild stretch of undercliff called The Floors, covered with thick undergrowth of gorse, bramble and bushes. You come across a number of such areas on the south Devon coast and they are a favourite haunt of birds, both resident and migrant. From mid-March to July listen for the songs of willow warbler and whitethroat and, perched on bushes, stonechats, goldfinches and yellowhammers. Overhead watch for kestrels and buzzards and, skimming over the hedges, sparrowhawks.

Coming down from West Down Beacon you may be able to see as far as Portland near Weymouth. The Path runs through some pinewoods and gorse along the boundary of the West Down Golf Course. Keep to the track nearest to the sea and it will bring you to the front at Budleigh Salterton.

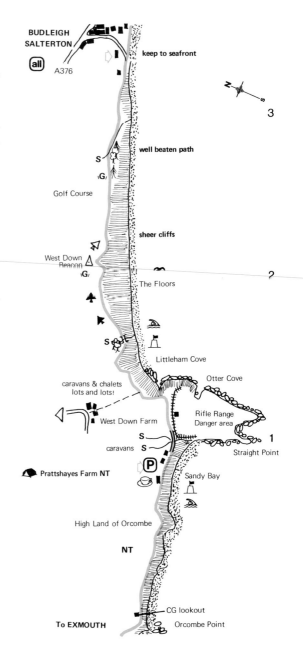

32

Walk 20 — Coastal Path

BUDLEIGH SALTERTON–LADRAM BAY

4¾ miles (7¾km); moderate

Cum. 93¾ miles (150¾km)

Budleigh Salterton (pop. 4500) is a small resort and its origins go back to the 13th century or earlier when the salt pans at the mouth of the Otter were worked. The steeply shelving beach is popular with collectors of coloured pebbles. The Victorian painter, Sir John Millais, painted his famous picture, *The Boyhood of Raleigh* here, with part of the sea wall as the setting.

Lying 1½ miles (2½km) inland is the charming village of East Budleigh, a wool port until the 15th century when the Otter began to silt up. Hays Barton, a Tudor farmhouse 1 mile (1½km) west was the birthplace of Sir Walter Raleigh in 1552.

*There is a short detour to cross the Otter. You cannot wade its mouth (except, perhaps, at very low tide and, **even then, take care**). For the detour, at the end of the promenade, take the footpath leading inland on the top of the embankment near the playing field. This will bring you to a bridge; cross the bridge and the cattle-grid on the drive up to South Farm. A Coast Path sign directs you along the edge of a wood (not down by the river).*

On reaching the cliff, the Path is straightforward and continues close to the cliff edge for 2½ miles (4km) through pleasant pasture and arable land until, in a wooded coombe running down to the sea, you come to the Ladram Bay caravan site.

On Ladram Bay beach there are two famous red sandstone pillars.

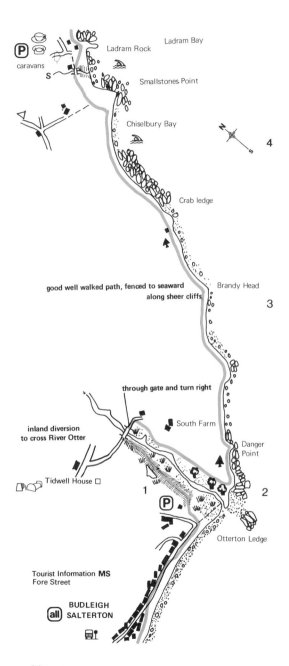

33

Walk 21 — Coastal Path
LADRAM BAY–SIDMOUTH–SALCOMBE HILL CLIFF
3½ miles (5½km); strenuous
Cum. 97¼ miles (156½km)

A Coast Path sign above the beach at Ladram directs you across fields past a pub, the Three Rocks (open in the summer), up the long climb of over 500 feet (150m) to the upper slopes of High Peak. The last stretch is pretty steep. The slopes are covered by a Forestry Commission conifer plantation. Unfortunately, the Path does not go to the top but runs round the crest. A clear Path leads down the other side and then climbs up a gorse-covered slope. At the top of the slope is a kissing-gate. Beyond this the Path descends through trees to the road running steeply into Sidmouth. There is a wide grass sward on which you can walk almost the whole way down to the front.

Sidmouth (pop. 12,000) has been a popular resort since the early 19th century. The young Princess (later Queen) Victoria spent the winter here with her parents in 1819 and many of the Georgian houses of that time still survive. There is an excellent sandy beach and many good pubs.

Cross the footbridge over the River Sid. There are steps and a Coast Path sign showing the way up to Salcombe Hill Cliff. The Path forks at a memorial when you reach the top of the hill; take the fork on the seaward side.

A left detour on a path bordered by trees via Springcombe avoids the very steep ascent of Dunscombe Cliff (see Walk 22).

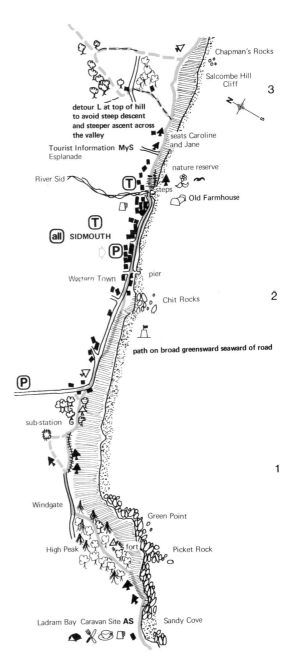

Chapman's Rocks

Salcombe Hill Cliff

3

detour L at top of hill
to avoid steep descent
and steeper ascent across
the valley

seats Caroline and Jane

Tourist Information MyS
Esplanade

nature reserve

River Sid

steps

Old Farmhouse

SIDMOUTH

pier

Western Town

Chit Rocks

2

path on broad greensward seaward of road

sub-station

1

Windgate

Green Point

High Peak

fort

Picket Rock

Ladram Bay Caravan Site **AS**

Sandy Cove

Walk 22 — Coastal Path
SALCOMBE HILL CLIFF–
BRANSCOMBE BEACH

3½ miles (5½km); strenuous
Cum. 100¾ miles (162km)

This section has two hard climbs (see maps 21 and 22 for less strenuous detour). As you come over Salcombe Hill Cliff and begin the descent down the other side of the wide combe running down to Salcombe Mouth, the prospect makes a fine view. The Path drops steeply to the beach to where the stream has cut a gully.

There are 130 steps down to the pebbly beach if you have the energy to climb back up!

Notice that the formation of the cliffs has changed. The red sandstone has given way to greensand and clays and later chalk.

From above the beach the Path climbs up the slope of the 500-foot (150m) Dunscombe Cliff. This is the beginning of National Trust land covering the coast to the village of Branscombe (see Walk 23).

The Path then turns slightly to negotiate Weston Combe and a steep pull out along the top of the 514-foot (160m) Weston Cliff. Approaching Coxe's Cliff, it veers inland a little until you join a farm track.

On the cliff edge here are traces of an Iron Age or Roman encampment.

Follow the farm track entering the wooded slopes on the left. On the right there are mounds from waste flints from former lime workings.

An alternative path zig-zags down the cliff face and climbs back again to rejoin the Path near Branscombe Mill.

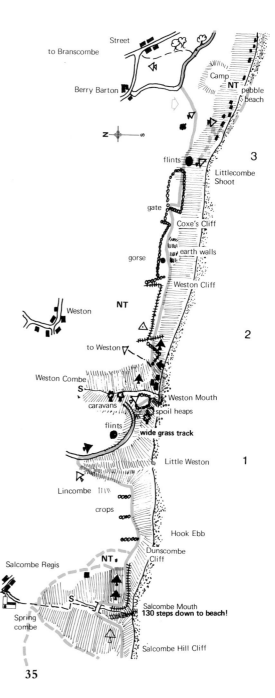

Walk 23 — Coastal Path

BRANSCOMBE BEACH– BEER–SEATON

4 miles (6½km); strenuous
Cum. 104¾ miles (168½km)

Branscombe, one of the most attractive villages in south Devon, is over 1000 years old. The estate was owned originally by King Alfred. The old church has traces of Saxon origin and the house opposite, known as Church Living was for visiting clerics. Parts of the house are 700 years old.

A road and a footpath lead inland off the Coast Path at Branscombe Mouth to the village and inn, the Mason's Arms; another path to the fine Branscombe Mill.

From Branscombe Mouth there are two official Coast Path routes: one climbs up the imposing slope of Hooken Cliff and along the top with splendid views. For the other you take the road close to the shore through bungalows and caravans. This becomes a winding footpath through humps and hollows and thick vegetation of the undercliff. In 1790 a landslip broke away 10 acres (25 hectares) of land, pushing back the shoreline 200 yards (180m). The landslip which revealed caves high in the cliffs is of great interest to naturalists.

The two Paths join at the top of Hooken Cliff and continue round the chalk outcrop of Beer Head, through fields then turning inland to join Little Lane. Continue past the Coast Guard station to Beer, a small and attractive former fishing village.

The Path continues through the ornamental gardens above the small beach and soon brings you to the outskirts of Seaton.

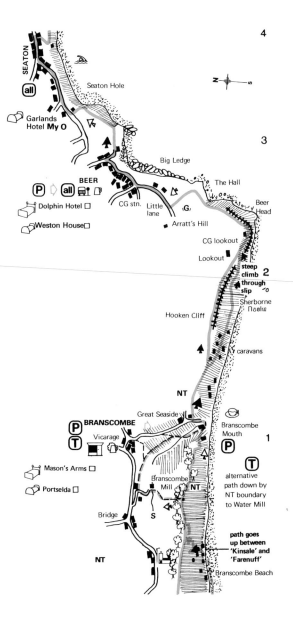

Walk 24 — Coastal Path
SEATON–
DOWLANDS LANDSLIP
3¾miles (6km); strenuous
Cum. 108½ miles (174½km)

Seaton (pop. 5500) is a small popular resort with a shelving shingle beach. Roman remains indicate it may have been the site of a port but in later times it was better known for its smuggling activities.

Seaton Electric Tramway runs a tram service from Seaton to Colyford and Colyton.

As will be seen from the map, this section covers about half of the famous Landslip which stretches for 5 (8km) of the 6 miles (9½km) between Seaton and Lyme Regis. Except for 1 mile (1½km) at the east (Lyme Regis) end, the Path is narrow; twisting, turning, dipping and climbing through what is probably one of the few areas of virgin forest in the British Isles. The Path becomes muddy and very slippery in wet weather. In any case, only those who are reasonably sure-footed should attempt to walk through. The only access for the public is at each end. Take with you any refreshments needed; there are no facilities en route. Leaflets on the Landslip are available at the Tourist Information offices at Seaton and Lyme Regis.

At the end of the promenade in Seaton cross the bridge over the River Axe. On the road, take the second drive on the right, that of the Axe Cliff Golf Club. The Coast Path follows this drive, past the club house and across part of the course, through a field-gate to a lane. Along here, a sign on the right directs you over fields. The Landslip entrance is across two stiles. This is a National Nature Reserve. You must keep to the marked Path; you cannot visit parts off the Path without a permit. Details from the Nature Conservancy, Roughmoor, Bishop's Hull, Taunton TA1 5AA.

See page 10 (Geology) for more details of the Landslip.

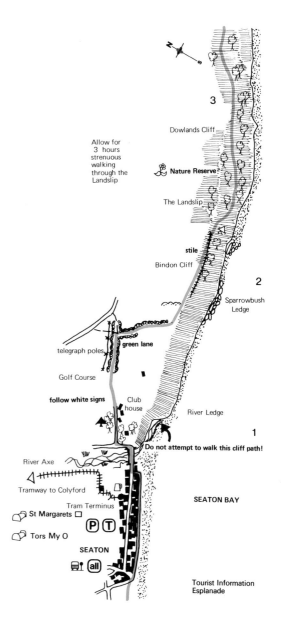

Allow for 3 hours strenuous walking through the Landslip

Dowlands Cliff

Nature Reserve

The Landslip

stile

Bindon Cliff

Sparrowbush Ledge

telegraph poles

green lane

Golf Course

follow white signs

Club house

River Ledge

Do not attempt to walk this cliff path!

River Axe

Tramway to Colyford

Tram Terminus

St Margarets

Tors My O

SEATON

SEATON BAY

Tourist Information
Esplanade

3

2

1

Walk 25 — Coastal Path
DOWLANDS LANDSLIP–
LYME REGIS

3½ miles (5½km); strenuous
Cum. 112 miles (180¼km)

This walk covers the east half of the Landslip Nature Reserve and the restrictions mentioned in the previous walk also apply. The Devon/Dorset border is just beyond the Landslip.

On emerging from the Landslip you follow a farm track above Underhill Farm and then a signposted Path across fields, bringing you out to a car park above the harbour at Lyme Regis.

Lyme Regis (pop. 3500) has a long history. Its 14th-century harbour, the Cobb, has been made famous by the book and film, *The French Lieutenant's Woman.* Lyme is mentioned in the Domesday Book and received its charter in 1284, regularly contributing ships and men in times of emergency, including the Armada. The ill-fated Duke of Monmouth landed here in 1685 to start his rebellion. Many Lyme citizens joined him and were executed.

One of Lyme's personalities was Mary Anning who, orphaned at ten years old, earned a living selling fossils she found. She became so famous that geologists wrote to her for specimens. She was granted a pension until she died in 1847. Mary Anning discovered the fossils of the ichthyosaurus, a previously unknown prehistoric marine animal. One of them is 21 feet (6½m) long and some of them are in the British Museum (Natural History) and the Geological Museum. The Philpot Museum in Lyme contains much of interest, both historical and geological.

Lyme Regis must be unique in the number of visitors, both young and old, seen walking about with geological hammers!

There is the old pub, the Royal Standard, on the Cobb.

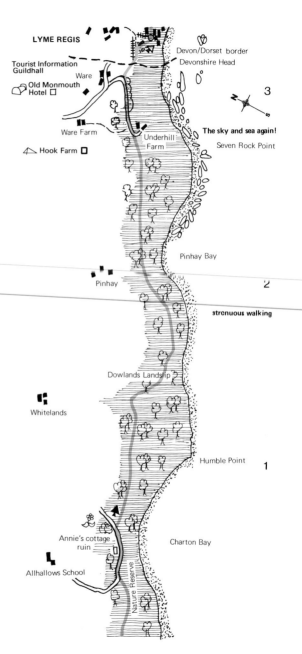

LYME REGIS

Tourist Information
Guildhall
Ware
Old Monmouth
Hotel □

Ware Farm

△ Hook Farm □

Devon/Dorset border
Devonshire Head

The sky and sea again!
Seven Rock Point

Underhill
Farm

3

Pinhay Bay

Pinhay

2

strenuous walking

Dowlands Landslip

Whitelands

Humble Point

1

Annie's cottage
ruin

Charton Bay

Allhallows School

Nature Reserve

BURRATOR GORGE AND MEAVY VALLEY

2¾ miles (4½ km) Very easy; muddy after rain

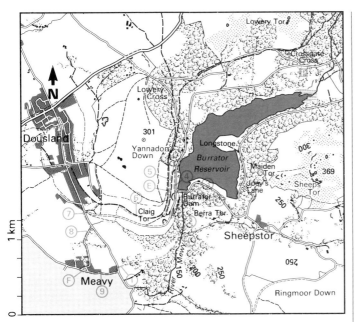

features in the valley. Its mighty slabs are cast about the hill below in spectacular fashion.

4 *Re-cross the dam; turn right; walk for 200 yds (183 m).*

D Above the left (west) roadside in a wooded glade is the cascading outflow of another leat - the Devonport, built in 1794.

5 *From the glade, follow a track, left, up the hillside to the site of Burrator Halt on the former GWR Yelverton-Princetown railway (closed 1956).*

E The view from the halt includes: Sharp, Lether and Down Tors, and Sheepstor village and church nestling beneath the brow of the great tor above.

6 *Follow the rail track around the south spur of Yannadon. The Burrator-Dousland road and the Plymouth leat are below while above is the Devonport (see also Walk 27). Leave the railroad at a curve and descend (left) to the cattle grid and road junction below.*

7 *The Plymouth leat passes beneath the Dousland road. Follow the Meavy road downhill for 200 yds (183 m) to a junction.*

8 *Turn right into Rectory Lane; pass the rectory gate, enter Meavy village centre at the Green.*

F The medieval church, rebuilt in the 15th century, was dedicated to St. Peter and consecrated in the year 1122. The Church House has become the Royal Oak Inn, its name derived from the celebrated, ancient relic outside its front door; under its branches is held the annual Meavy Oak Fair in June.

9 *Follow the road eastward through the village to reach the start.*

This walk passes through a very attractive piece of south west Dartmoor borderland and involves very little climbing. The ancient name of the river dammed at Burrator to supply Plymouth's water is Mew or Mewy. Its fine lower reach is easily accessible. Park at the roadside opposite Meavy School at the east end of the village.

1 *Walk through the gateway beside the old smithy (now called 'Moor View') and follow the woodland path, which crosses the former Meavy mill leat.*

A Sheepstor Brook joins the river in the gorge and the massive granite wall of the dam is seen through the trees. The remains of the mill-leat weir are below, and on the hillside

above the path, left, is the dry channel of the historic Plymouth leat, built by Sir Francis Drake in 1589 to carry drinking water to the city of Plymouth.

2 *Follow the path up to the leat, and then to the road above. Turn right, cross the dam and enjoy the prospect of the tors reflected in the lake.*

B The reservoir (completed 1898) made the Plymouth leat redundant. Conspicuous heights above the lake's further shore extend from Peak Hill to Cramber Down.

3 *At the east end of the dam, mount a flight of steps (right) and follow a steep path (left) to a rockpile.*

C Berra Tor ('beara' - a wood, the tor in the wood) gives its name in the form 'Burrator' to several

---

BLACK TOR and the UPPER MEWY VALLEY

2½ miles (4 km) Easy; dry

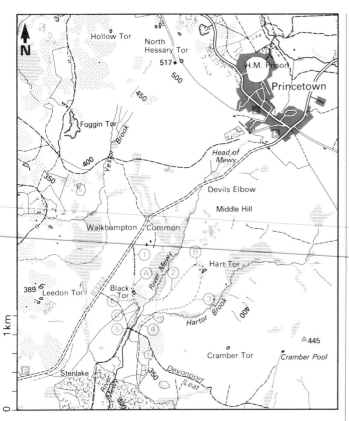

This attractive piece of country near Princetown is easily reached. Take the Yelverton-Princetown road (B3212) for one and a half miles (2.4 km) beyond Goadstone Pond, a small sheet of water (right) on the crest of the moorland escarpment. Parking space may be found on either side of the road.

1 *Follow the clear path from the parking space to the tor, which rises due south of the road.*

A Black Tor has two piles; at the smaller is a huge logan stone pivoted on its base; it could be rocked until recent years: a large pear-shaped basin lies on its upper face. The larger pile has a rockface on its east side, and an interior rock-chimney. Descend to the valley, cross the River Mewy at Black Tor Ford and make for the stone rows ahead.

2 *On the left (east) bank a double row leads to a burial cairn at the foot of Hart Tor; parallel to it, a much ruined single row also leads to a*

burial cairn. Each cairn has a retaining circle. Climb to Hart Tor.

B The tor heads a considerable clitter and has a large area of granite bedding on the summit. The river disappears southwards below conifer-clad hillsides between Lether and Sheeps Tors and the stream flowing around the east/south foot of the tor takes its name - Hartor Brook.

3 *Follow the brook downstream to an enclosed Bronze Age village; the pound entrance retains the original paving and the huts have protective entrance passages, once roofed.*

4 *Walk downstream to see the cascading Devonport leat on Raddick Hill, and aqueducted across the River Mewy - a delightful spot known as Iron Bridge.*

5 *Cross the river and walk upstream past the numerous pits and mounds left by medieval tinners, to reach Black Tor Hole.*

C Central in the dell is a twisting waterfall beneath rowan trees where Mewy creates a deep pool. On both river banks is the ruin of a blowing house, each in use until the mid-17th century, the tin processed here being marketed in the stannary town of Tavistock. Each house contains mortar stones, and its leat from the river is traceable. On the remaining door-lintel of the left bank house is inscribed the Roman numeral 'XIII' (13), being the registered number in stannary records of the house.

6 *A zigzag path leads from the dell to the tor above; follow this to the start. Notice as you walk the weird outline of Leedon Tor three quarters of a mile (1.2 km) to the west.*

40

BIRCH TOR, CHALLACOMBE, VITIFER MINE

2½ miles (4 km) Moderately easy; dry. DANGER: flooded water-wheel pits

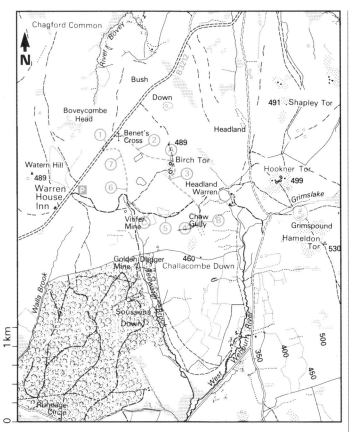

left and pass the corner of an enclosure; cross two gerts (the banks are
very steep); beyond the second, follow
a narrow branch path, left, to the tor
above.

A Birch Tor has several piles. Go
first to the highest placed (north)
pile and see the view of north-east
Dartmoor. From the southern main
pile, look down into the valley of
Redwater Brook containing the
ruined buildings of the Birch Tor &
Vitifer Mine and, further downstream, those of the Golden
Dagger; Challacombe Down rises
directly ahead.

3 *Walk towards the left side of
Challacombe Down. Cross the
Vitifer-Headland miners' path and
notice the buildings of the former
Headland Warren, left. Cross the
heads of two gerts to a group of
standing stones.*

B Challacombe Down triple stone
row is a compact monument with a
blocking stone at the higher end and
the site of a grave at the lower. The
kistvaen has disappeared, but the retaining circle remains. Signs exist in
mid-row of a second grave.

4 *Return to the miners' path.*

5 *Descend left to the Redwater valley.*

C From the brink of Chaw Gully
(left) peer into this 50 ft (15 m) deep
gash in the dynamite-torn hillside.

6 *On reaching the ruined mine buildings follow the path beside Redwater
Brook.* CAUTION: *it skirts the edge
of a dangerous wheel pit.*

7 *When the path crosses the head of a
gert, Benet's Cross and the car park
come into sight. Return direct to the
start.*

The Birch Tor & Vitifer Tine Mine
continued to work, albeit in
diminishing spasms, until the early
1930s, having provided employment
for several generations of miners
from Dartmoor hamlets and border-
country villages. The scenery of the
district is very striking, comprising
rugged tors, mining gerts blasted by
gunpowder and later dynamite and
the sweeping backcloth of the
Hameldon ridge. Take the B3212

east from Two Bridges or west from
Moretonhampstead. Use a car park
(south side of road) ½ mile (0.8km)
east of Warren House Inn. Heed any
path diversion signs.

1 *Walk 150 yds (137 m) along the
road to Benet's Cross, weather-beaten
boundary mark (right). The incised
letters 'WB' indicate 'Warren
Bounds', (ie Headland Warren).*

2 *Follow a descending green path joining with one from the car park. Turn*

CATOR COMMON AND PIZWELL ANCIENT TENEMENT
2 miles (3¼ km) Very easy; dry

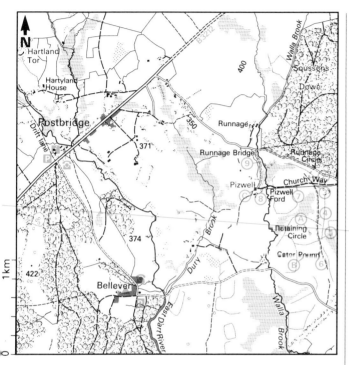

is Church Way - and enters a gate beside a 'Bridle path' fingerpost.

4 *For a short deviation, stay on the public right of way over Cator Common, noticing a distinct mound on the hill crest on the right.*

A The mound is the base of a cairn that once was raised over an interment; the central hollow formerly contained the kistvaen. Removal of the cairn has revealed a fine retaining circle of some 25 remaining stones. The lack of height here does not diminish the pleasing and clearly defined view over the central basin.

5 *The route is followed a little further until some set stones come into view. These form the wall of*

B Cator Pound, a rectangular enclosure of great antiquity, which was approached by a droveway on the south-west side.

6 *Retrace the route to the gate (Note 3).*

7 *Turn left into Church Way; cross Walla Brook at Pizwell Ford.*

C Pizwell. Walk between the buildings, then return and re-cross Walla Brook. The lowest placed building of the tenement is a medieval longhouse which, now in use as a store, was occupied until 1935.

8 *Either - return along Church Way and cross the common towards the opening in the trees and the start.*

9 *Or - follow the pleasant right bank of Walla Brook upstream to Runnage Bridge, turning right at the road ro reach the start.*

Dartmoor's medieval history is uniquely represented by the splendid group of buildings at Pizwell in the central basin, the originals of a tenement cluster of three farms documented in 1260. Although nowadays, due to cost, tin or slate has replaced thatch, all the buildings are almost as they were. Even the ford and the stepping stones over Walla Brook (a tributary of East Dart) and the stony road approaching the ford between the heather banks remains unaffected by modern trends. The road is the ancient Church Way between Pizwell and Widecombe-in-the-Moor.

Branch right from the B3212 one mile (1.6 km) east of Postbridge Post Office, at the sign 'Widecombe'. Cross Walla Brook at Runnage Bridge and continue half a mile (0.8 km) ahead to an opening in the Soussons plantations, left. Park on the wide grass verge.

1 *In the opening is an almost perfect Bronze Age retaining circle, with two side-stones of the central kistvaen still in place.*

2 *Cross the common opposite towards the cone of Bellever Tor (seen above the Bellever plantations). At a wide transverse track, turn left.*

3 *The track intersects a stony road - this*

BENJY TOR

2½ miles (4 km) Very easy; dry

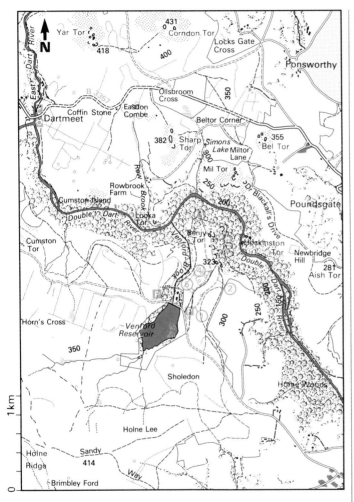

2 *On reaching a banked-up leat, follow it (left) and continue parallel to the nearby Stoke corn-ditch wall, right. The rock-crowned mound of Benjy Tor will appear ahead; walk near the wall in approaching the tor in order to avoid a large bracken field, left.*

A Benjy Tor consists of several piles on a rock-ridge 500 yds (457 m) in length, and provides striking views into the Double Dart Gorge; the scenic Dr Blackall's Drive appears on the opposite brink zig-zagging under rugged Mil Tor and passing above Hockinston Tor. Sharp Tor rises to break the outlines of Yar and Corndon Tors. From the larger of the two north piles, its rockface falling precipitously to the river, one sees in detail Mil Tor and the valley of Simon's Lake as well as the straight trough of Row Brook and the roofs of Rowbrook Farm further up the valley.

3 *Walk to the smaller north pile; double back, left, and follow a clear path below the west side of the rock-ridge.*

B The tributary valley of Venford Brook is below, right. Beyond it, notice the marks of long-disused medieval enclosures on the moor, backed by the lofty Holne Ridge.

4 *The path passes through bracken and joins a broad, grass path coming down from the south pile. Turn right into this.*

5 *Take the left fork to the car park (a right fork would take you to the reservoir). Water seen foaming into the reservoir on the further bank is piped from the small Swincombe reservoir.*

Many of Dartmoor's most attractive features lie hidden from the casual eye. In approaching Benjy Tor from the west there is no hint of the breath-taking spectacle to come. It is an exciting tor for children, easily climbable and with crevices and carverns which can be seen on the summit plateau not too near the brink of the gorge. Take the Holne-Hexworthy road to the east side of Venford reservoir; car park, left.

1 *Follow a green path uphill from the back of the car park.*

STALDON (pronounced 'Stahldon')

5 miles (8 km) Moderately easy; gradual climb 405 ft (123 m); dry

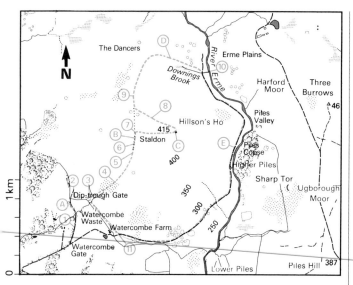

row's east side there is an inter-mediate grave and near the fifth to the end stone on the west side a remnant kistvaen and another grave.

7 *Leave the row at the intermediate kistvaen and cross the moor (right) in line with the cairn-crowned dome of Three Burrows; the highest hill of the further valley-side range. Walk towards large stone cairn ahead.*

C Staldon Burrow and Hillson's House. The angular appearance of this large Bronze Age cairn is due to the enterprising, if eccentric behaviour of a clock-maker recluse, named Hillson. He retreated here in the early 1800s, built the house and made eight-day clocks.

8 *From Hillson's House, return to the stone row by making (right) for the tallest stones.*

9 *From the end of the row descend the hill due north and pass round the con-tour (left) of a tributary valley-head, to walk down -*

D Downing's Brook valley. Near where this swift little stream meets the Erme, on the left bank is a fine example of a Dartmoor medieval tinners' cache. Built entirely of stone corbelling, with a domed roof, of a type known as a 'beehive hut'.

10 *A stony track crosses Downing's Brook in a dip below the beehive hut.*

E Piles Copse. Seen from the Erme valley floor is this huge canopy of oaks on the opposite, steep hillside under Sharp Tor, one of the pri-meval oak groves unique to Dart-moor.

11 *When the track reaches the Water-works gate, leave it and walk over the moor (right) beside the enclosure wall. Cross Redaven Lake, return to the start at Dip-trough Gate.*

The massive hill of Staldon forms the west side of the deep Erme valley, over which, and southward to the sea, there are excellent views. The hill is topped by a Bronze Age cairn, with one of the most ef-fectively sited stone rows in Europe nearby. Drive north from Corn-wood to Vicarage Bridge over the River Yealm. Cross; turn right. Take the first turning left, between houses, then immediately right. Drive through Watercombe Waste Gate and park away from the tracks. The notice 'Permitted Path to the Moor' means that no rights of way and parking exist, but that the farmer owning the Waste permits both to considerate visitors who close gates and leave no litter.

1 *Follow the track through -*

A Watercombe Waste. The ancient track, beside which flows the Blachford leat, is overshadowed by -hollies, oaks, ashes, elms and beeches. The leat flows from Redaven Lake at the ford. Beyond it, left, is Dip-trough Gate and the old Watercombe sheep dip.

2 *Beyond Dip-trough Gate leave the track and follow the wall of the Waste, right.*

3 *At the wall-corner walk up the wide, shallow Redaven Gulf past a small rockfield and above it, another wider one.*

4 *When the rockfield becomes dense you will see above left the lower end of Staldon Row.*

5 *Make for the lowest, massive ter-minal stone of the row.*

6 *Follow the row.*

B Staldon Stone Row. The dramatic effect of this row on the hillcrest can be seen from the hills east of the Erme valley. On the

44

Walk 32 — Dartmoor

HEY TOR, QUARRIES AND GRANITE TRAMROAD

2½ miles (4 km) Very easy; dry

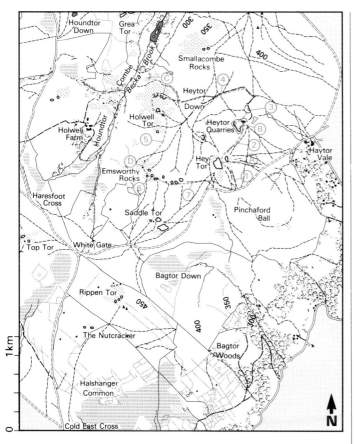

The huge granite bosses of High ('Hey' in the vernacular) Tor, are a notable landmark from the sea, moorland and the east Devon heathlands. Easy to reach it is a popular tor with tourists. Below it on the north side are the quarries from which granite was extracted in 1825 for the foundation stone of London Bridge. This travelled in horse-drawn trucks down the unique granite tramroad to the Stover Canal for shipment at Teignmouth Quay; a milestone in Dartmoor's industrial history. Take the Bovey Tracey-Widecombe road to the car park south of the road on the crest of Heytor Down.

1 *Follow the broad path to the tor.*

A Hey Tor has a large rock basin reached by steps cut in the rock of the east pile; do not use them in a high wind. Stand below the east pile's immense rock-wall where trial holes have been drilled in the granite.

2 *Follow a path directly in front of the rock-wall, descending through heather to the corner of a wire fence; notice the line of the tramroad on the flank of Heytor Down ahead. Descend and enter the quarry.*

B Heytor Quarry. The harshness of the quarry face is softened by heather and gorse, which in high summer is extremely colourful on the surrounding moorland, and by the water of Heytor Ponds. Notice the remaining wooden beam and iron winch of the crane.

3 *Follow the tramroad track from the quarry (granite rail sets will soon appear in the turf) to a set of junction 'points'.*

4 *Follow the main line westward (left), through a shallow cutting and down to its terminus -*

C Holwell Quarry. A sheer working face, a crane-base and ruined buildings speak of intense industry here 160 years ago. Climb Holwell Tor above the quarry and look over Houndtor Combe to Grea Tor and Great Hound Tor.

5 *Cross a hollow in the hillside towards -*

D Emsworthy Rocks. Here are two more quarries of the Heytor complex, one at either end of a long rock-ridge where branch lines of the railroads terminate.

6 *Follow the crest of the Emsworthy rock-ridge and notice the second quarry.*

7 *Follow a green path joining the Bovey Tracey road at Heytor car park.*

GREAT HOUND AND GREA TORS

2½ miles (4 km) Very easy; dry

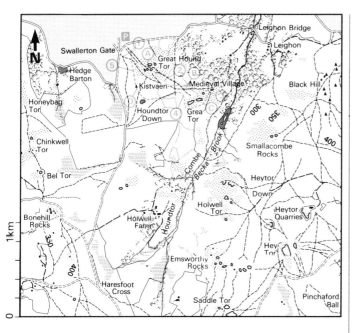

'Houndtor' should properly be 'Great Hound Tor', for there is a 'Little Hound Tor' on the north moor. It is the centre of an area of superstition and legend - even its name may have sprung from the legendary, spectral black hound of Dartmoor encountered on the tor as recently as 1965. Like Hey Tor, it is easily reached and there is a car park at Swallerton Gate (near the former 'Houndtor Inn'). Great Hound Tor is the gateway to an area rich in natural, unspoilt beauty, with Grea Tor and Houndtor Combe forming its centre-piece. Take the Chagford-Ashburton road to Swallerton Gate, one and a half miles (2.4 km) south of Heatree Cross and turn into the car park.

1 *Follow the broad path to the tor.*
A Great Hound Tor, a natural granite citadel, is a double 'avenue' tor, where Ice Age weathering has removed decayed rock to form parallel avenues between remaining rockpiles, of which the northern is most impressive. Walk through this, observing the cavities, pillars, shelves and gargantuan blocks on either side. At the far end of the avenue the heights above Houndtor Combe appear beyond Grea Tor; below, in a dip near Grea Tor, are the outlines of ruined buildings.
2 *Follow the path to the buildings, the remains of -*
B Houndtor Down medieval village. Excavation has revealed a settlement of 11 buildings, probably

pre-Conquest in origin when houses were of wattle and turf. Some are longhouses, some auxiliary buildings; several houses show traces of fireplaces, and one has an entrance passage with a cooler (a chamber built into the wall facing north-east to avoid sunlight). Like so many longhouses on the Moor, these are likely to have been emptied by the scourge of the Black Death in 1348. The situation of this village is not merely beautiful, but dramatic.
3 *Walk from the village to the lowest pile (left) of -*
C Grea Tor. There are in all five piles, increasing proportionately in size and elevation. Notice the contrasting sheet-like masses of aplite in the largest pile and the prevailing, coarse-grained granite of the others. The view across Houndtor Combe is of Holwell Tor rising to fine effect.
4 *Return towards Great Hound Tor; turn left into a clear, transverse track to the crest of Houndtor Down. Fork right to pass north (right) of a small tarn (sometimes dry); walk north-west to standing stones ahead.*
D Houndtor Down kistvaen. Had not the road-makers a century ago, rifled the kistvaen for stones, which they are known to have done, this would have been a striking monument; now, the west segment of the retaining kerb-cicle (one with the stones close-set), the cover-stone and one side-stone have disappeared. The two prominent tors seen west of the road are, left to right, Chinkwell and Honeybag.
5 *Return over the moor to the now visible car park.*

46

GER TOR AND TAVY CLEAVE

3½ miles (5½ km) Some rough, wet ground; 450 ft (137 m) climb from start

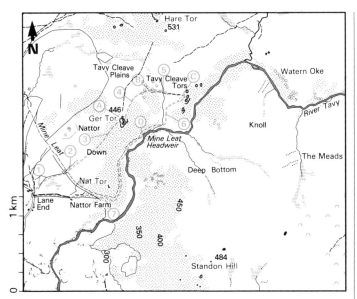

The area lies in the Willsworthy live-firing range, where firing is frequent, except during August; check the firing programme before setting out. West Dartmoor's Tavy is the second swiftest river in Britain, second only that is, to Spey in the Cairngorms, Scotland. Its swift current is due to it making a descent of 1000 ft (305 m) in only eight miles (12.8 km). Tavy has cut a rugged, impressive gorge over the ages; treeless and rockbound, it is known as Tavy Cleave. From the A386 Tavistock-Okehampton road turn right at Mary Tavy War Memorial four and a quarter miles (6.8 km) from Tavistock then take the first left turning, signposted 'HORNDON' and continue to Lane End (where the tarmac road ends); cross the cattle grid and park on open ground near the military flagpole. Do not obstruct any track.

1 *Walk towards Ger Tor, at the head of Nattor Down.*

2 *Cross the Mine leat bridge; (the leat once supplied the water-wheels of a large copper mine at Mary Tavy, but now runs to Kingsett Down hydroelectric plant).*

3 *Remain on the track until near the hill-crest, then make for a clear, grassy patch near rocks ahead.*

A View from upper, north-west side of tor: this possesses a grandeur not common on British moorlands. Below, Tavy leaves its cleave with an audible roar, Vur Tor and the ridges of the northern fen appear in the east, and Standon raises its bulk beyond the river.

4 *Cross the tract of level ground towards Hare Tor's summit cone; this is*

Tavy Cleave Plains. *When near the stones of a hut village below, right; descend to it.*

B The first hut, right, has original door jambs and a step into the interior (floor then was at least 2 ft (0.6 m) lower). Cross the village towards Sharp Tor above the rock-ridge ahead and visit another hut with exceptionally good door jambs. Stand within the doorway and appreciate the wonderful prospect.

5 *Make for the ford in the tributary valley ahead; the path continues to a wide gap in the rocks of Sharp Tor. Avoid the gap and bear right to a cleft in the middle of the main pile.*

C On reaching 'Tavy Cleave Sharp' walk close under the rock and look through the cleft for the view.

6 *Descend to the main valley, by returning to the tributary ford and following the stream downwards. Although difficult in places, this is not to be compared with the ground that would be encountered in a direct walk from Sharp Tor to the river.*

D The Mine leat and its headweir are visible below. A rough path follows the river bank to the weir at the foot of the cleave; from the weir follow the leatside path, which eventually curves below the rocks of Nat Tor to cross Nattor Down.

7 *Leave the leat beyond the bend and follow a grass path down to the entrance gate of Nattor farm (left), then take the farm road to Lane End and the start.*

47

A RAILROAD WALK - PLYMOUTH & DARTMOOR RAILWAY: GWR

4½ miles (7¼ km) Moderately easy; some uneven grass moor

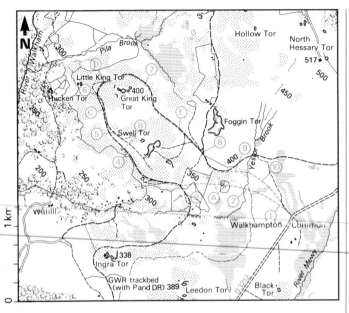

England's only mountain railway (Yelverton-Princetown) was closed by Dr Beeching in 1956. Built in 1881, it used most of the trackbed of an earlier line, the Plymouth & Dartmoor Railway (P & DR), a horse-truck tramroad (opened 1823) for transporting granite for shipment on the Plym estuary from Sir Thomas Tyrwhitt's quarries near Princetown. The serpentine, finely engineered track passes over rocky moorland and offers exceptional views over western Dartmoor. Take the Yelverton-Princetown road (B3212) for about one and a half miles (2.7 km) beyond Goadstone Pond. Park in the small disused quarry (left) near a right-hand bend.

1 *Walk towards the jagged quarry-head of Swell Tor.*

2 *Cross a flowing leat and descend to the valley of Yestor Brook among tin works; continue in the same direction to a Bronze Age village with associated pounds. The main enclosure wall has a paved north-east entrance; some huts have entrance passages and standing door jambs.*

A Viewpoint: southward rise Leedon Tor and Ingra Tor; the GWR trackbed runs below Ingra Tor. The deviating P & DR crosses the brook on an arch-bridge. The transition between moorland, border-country, lowlands, Tamar valley and east Cornwall seen from here, is very pleasing.

3 *The united railroad lines curve below the hut village. Walk through two broken walls (250 yds/229 m apart) to the rail track.*

4 *In a short way leave the rail track and walk to a row of large, shaped granite objects near Swell Tor.*

B Swell Tor Quarry supplied stone for several early 19th century London buildings, including Nelson's column and parts of London Bridge. The P & DR siding was later adopted by the GWR; alongside are some redundant spare corbels cut in 1903 for London Bridge, but never shipped.

5 *Follow the siding to the main line.*

C Another siding and an inclined plane appear ahead under Great King Tor.

6 *The siding is based on the P & DR main line near the GWR deviation and bridge over a moorland track. The GWR enters a cutting on the spur of King Tor; the P & DR is blocked by the GWR embankment and reappears beyond. Follow it.*

D The P & DR rounds the King Tor spur on a hillside ledge, where the view of the Walkham valley is very fine. On the grassy curve of the trackbed are three iron rail-chairs of 1823 still in position.

7 *The two lines unite beyond the cutting; follow the track to the Swell Tor-Foggin Tor col.*

E From Foggin Tor Quarry (left), came granite for Sir Thomas Tyrwhitt's Napoleonic war prison at Princetown.

8 *Follow the track until the prehistoric village (Note A) appears below (right).*

9 *Leave the track; keeping above the village, make for the Yestor valley.*

10 *Return to the start.*

48